He Said, "Press":
Hearing God Through Grief

By

Patti McCarthy Broderick

WITH A TEN WEEK BIBLE STUDY

Scripture taken from the HOLY BIBLE, NEW
INTERNATIONAL VERSION ®. Copyright ©
1973,1978,1984 by International Bible Society. Used by
permission of Zondervan Publishing House. All rights
reserved.

Library of Congress Control Number: 2003098737

ISBN: 0-9747557-0-2

Additional copies of this book are available at
www.hesaidpress.com

Printed in the USA by
Morris Publishing
3212 East Highway 30
Kearney, NE 68847
1-800-650-7888

Dedicated to the memory of
Mark Patrick McCarthy
26 Oct 63 – 26 Jan 95
For the beautiful imprint he left on my life.

The Imprint

The imprint left from a life well lived,
Imbeds itself deeply in the soul,
Replicating the uniqueness of the life,
Forged by sweet memories,
Forever a source of beauty and joy.

The imprint left is indelible,
Impacting every arena of life,
Teaching the urgency of love,
Leaving those blessed by the imprint,
Forever changed in marvelous ways.

January 1999

iii

Contents

Poem Index

Acknowledgements

A special thanks to:

Deb Jackson Carter, a fellow widow who encouraged me to "get those poems out there."

Linda Dillow, my mentor, my encourager and my friend. For your example of faithfulness.

Mary Ellen MacGregor, expert in the English language, my editor and my aunt. For your expertise, your time and your patience.

To my new husband, Terry. Without your funding, and belief in me, this book would not have come to be.

To my God. Thank you for allowing me to be Your imperfect ambassador. May You be honored with the words on these pages.

Dear Reader,

As I look back over the events of my life, they seem surreal, as though I am reading a novel about someone else's life. The pain that was once an unbearably deep sucking chest wound is now only a memory of that pain. Although God undoubtedly used time to mend that wound, the real healing came from God's very presence. During a time when He dealt me a blow that sent me reeling on my heels, he was also there to catch me as no one else could have. But I had to trust Him when He seemed least trustworthy. During my emotional tumble, I held tighter and listened more intently to God than I ever had before. Like a child with his face pressed up against a window, I sought to find God in the midst of my confusion and understand what He was seeing. The joy He brought in my life and the hope His truths infused in my soul are a testimony that He is worth listening to. I did not do things right all the time, but each time I *chose* to press into the Right One, the evidence of His power mounted. I am convinced that if psychiatrists could harness the contentment I found by pressing into God, that it would be their most prescribed drug. But it is not as easy as swallowing a pill. It is a day to day struggle to overcome our own flesh and seek God.

As the years have passed, I have become overwhelmed with the number of men and women facing similar, tragic circumstances. Not all I run across are widows and widowers, but parents who have lost children, divorcees who have lost a marriage, adults who have lost a childhood, and the afflicted who have lost their health. The common thread I can relate to through them all is the great pain and grief in this life. Often, the pain becomes crippling and the loss incapacitating. I want to minister to them all; to point them to the truths God has taught me through my pain and to *"comfort those in any trouble with the comfort we ourselves have received from God"* (2Cor 1:4).

Hence this book: a writing to record the events of this tumultuous era in my life while they remain a vivid memory; a writing to remember and acknowledge the faithfulness of God to His Word; a writing to minister to my burdened, hurting fellow sufferers; and a writing to challenge all who venture through this journey called "life" to stand firm on the truths of God and His Word and to press ahead knowing our trustworthy God is by our side.

This book is not written to become an end in itself. It will not answer all or most of the questions you or your loved one may be struggling with now. Rather, it was written as a beginning, to point you to the One who does have all the answers, the Mighty Comforter, the Great I Am. This is a testimony of my walk through some rough roads of life while continually attempting to lean on the Great Comforter, to trust Him and to bathe myself in the living waters of His Word. It chronicles my journey as I have tried to get off the throne and let God be God, to free Him to work powerfully in my life, as only He can do.

May you sense God's loving presence in real and physical ways as you read this book. Let Him hold you as He longs to do as you press into His loving, capable arms.

Patti

Press

Lord, I admit it is hard to press on
When it seems what I desire most is behind me.
I long for the love of a man You've taken home.
A man You gave me, and then took away all too soon.

Like a horse with a bit, You guide me where I need to go.
But I can't move ahead when I'm looking over my shoulder.
So I strain to look ahead, even if I'm not sure where we're going.
I choose to follow Your lead because I know You.

Often, the road before me seems rough, even impassable.
And I'm not always sure why You've chosen this path,
Yet, You are there, gently speaking words of encouragement.
And our relationship is all that I need.

So I press ahead, with my ears listening for Your voice.
Knowing that all else will fade away, but You will never leave me.
I heard Your voice clearly in my love's last word spoken,
He did not say "look back" nor even "remember." He said, "Press."

January 26, 1996

About this Book

"Press." It was the last word he would ever speak. The word has echoed through my head over and over as I have searched for its meaning. I felt as though God had spoken directly to me through Mark's last word. In the early days after Mark's death, the word roused me to "press on." It encouraged me to put one feeble foot in front of the other; to get up in the morning; to continue brushing my teeth; to smile at my children. As time went on, "press" came to signify my need to "press up," to lean on God in ways I had never done before, to put aside my doubts and stand firmly on God's Word. I could see that my only hope for real faith, strength and perspective, came from God's hand. In later years, "press" came to mean "press in," to become more through my widowhood. God wanted me to do more than endure; He wanted me to become more Christ-like in character by persevering, to look for God's bigger purpose in my situation and even to embrace my lot in life.

The strength I found to "press on," "press up" and "press in" during each phase of my widowhood came from an intimate relationship with God. As I deliberately pressed into my trusted Confidant, Counselor and Friend, He became this young widow's refuge in the midst of the storm we all face, called life.

Section One:

Press On

Oh Lord, he's deploying…again.
How can this be? He just came back, it seems.
I want to do right by You this time, God, and by him.
But I need Your help, Lord.
It's so hard.

As he prepares to go, keep me from distancing myself from him so it won't hurt so much.
I know that will only make me regret the way we spent our time together when he's gone.
Instead, Lord, give me the courage to savor each moment we're together,
As if it were the last, forever.

As he goes, help me not show bitterness or anger toward him.
Remind me that it's all right for him to see how sad I am that he's leaving.
Let my children see my sadness is genuine, but it's OK to talk about it.
Help me neither cling to him, nor push him away as he goes.
Let the last words from my lips be words of love for him.

While he's gone, I pray, oh Lord, for strength.
I wasn't built to be alone or to be a single parent and it's not easy.
Give me strength to keep busy so I won't be tempted to have a pity party.
Give me strength to put the kids to bed when it's best for them, not when it's best for me.
Help me to be patient with the kids when they act out, it's hard on them too.

2

When they cry out for Daddy, keep my tongue from a bitter reply about his absence,

But rather help me answer with a gentle (and honest), "I miss Daddy too."

When the illnesses come, and everything mechanical breaks down,

As is always the case when he's gone, give me the courage to ask for help if I need it.

Even though I hate to go to bed without him,

Give me the wisdom to know when I need rest so I can face each day well rested.

Keep me, Lord from making snide remarks, especially within earshot of my kids,

About how much fun he's having,

And how great life must be free from the responsibilities of children.

Help me to remember how hard it would be to be separated from my spouse and my kids,

Especially if Jr. took his first step without me.

As I hustle about trying to accomplish the work of two adults,

Lord, remind me to take time out for my kids —

To hug them, to play with them, to listen to them, to wrestle with them

So that they feel secure in my love during this insecure time without a daddy around.

When he calls, Lord, give me the strength to tell him about things without whining.

Let me take the time to ask how things are for him, so he knows I care.

Help me bite my tongue when he talks of boredom, hours at the gym,

Or the inefficient maid he has in his hotel room.

When he asks to speak to the kids,

Help me remember that I would be longing to hear their sweet voices,

3

And to know they hadn't forgotten me, if I was away from them.
Lord, even though the thought of an adulterous affair seems almost comical to me,
Let me remember to say these words of reassurance to him, "I'm being faithful to you."
Let the last words from my lips be words of love for him.

When he returns, help me Lord, to make it a memorable homecoming for him.
May I resist the temptation to be jealous of the attention the little ones are getting.
Let me try to imagine how awful it must feel to be a stranger in my own home,
So that I remember to do my best to make him feel at home again.
Grant me the strength and the wisdom, oh Lord,
To let my husband return to his prior place in the family gradually.
Help me to neither throw every responsibility on him all at once,
Nor to withhold his responsibilities for myself to show him I can do them without his help.

Through it all, Lord, remind me I don't have to do it alone.
Let me continually seek your counsel.
When I fail, Lord, give me the humility to recognize my failure
And to seek out those I've wronged — my husband, my kids or You — to seek forgiveness.
Help me remember I am never really alone,
Help me to bask in the goodness of your love.
And may I wear out the knees of my pants in prayer to You.

May 1994

4

Chapter 1

Pressure Points:
God's Fingerprints

"Jesus said to them, 'My Father is always at His work to this very day, and I, too, am working.'" John 5:17

Feeling nauseous with the stomach flu, I stumbled to the kitchen, miserable. But Mark's sweet act of love somehow managed to transcend my physical anguish. He had attempted to clean the kitchen to my standards, far beyond those Mark deemed necessary. As I perused the makeshift, but quaint kitchen in the Italian villa that we called "home," I felt a sense of contentment despite the nausea. God's fingerprints were all over the path it had taken to get us to this place.

Pressure Points

When I was young, my five siblings and I infrequently had the opportunity to go to a nice restaurant for Sunday dinner. Unable to grasp the significance of the privilege, occasionally my siblings and I acted less than respectably. I can still feel the bruise as the hand of one of my parents grabbed me by the arm firmly and painfully and moved me to where I needed to go, whether it was to the car for a spanking or to the bathroom for "a good talking to." I liken much of my growth in Christ to God doing the same for me. I can look back and see the benefit of my parents' not allowing me to run amuck in a restaurant. Similarly, I can look back and see many times when God painfully grabbed my arm and moved me, not necessarily where I wanted, but where I needed to be.

First Taste of Humble Pie

Such was the case when I strode blithely and naively off to the Air Force Academy for college. My parents recall my entry as one of the hardest things they ever had to do. My father, a Virginia Military Institute graduate, knew what was in store for his daughter, and my mother could not get over the irony of having to leave her daughter under the "Bring Me Men" ramp at the Air Force Academy. But God's fingerprints were suspiciously all over what was to follow. "Humble" was not an adjective one would have used to describe me at that point in life. The valedictorian of my high school class, I was also voted "most athletic" by my classmates. However, the military delights in taking someone like me with a high self esteem to break her down so that she can be rebuilt not as an individual, but as a vital fighting unit, dependent on and fiercely loyal to her comrades in arms. But God had a higher purpose for putting my nose in the dirt. *If we are unable to humble ourselves, God graciously does it for us.*

God humbled me that first year at the Air Force Academy and there, with my face in the dirt, I had no where to look but up. On my knees at an Officers' Christian Fellowship retreat during my freshman year, I was humbled enough finally to see my need for a Savior. As long as I was a god in my own eyes, I did not need one. I definitely was not a god at the Air Force Academy; there, I was profoundly average. So I desperately needed to find my worth outside of my abilities. In Jesus, I found I was loved because of my inabilities as well as my abilities. In a world where there is always someone smarter, faster,

6

stronger and more gifted, I found it heartening to realize that the Master Designer, who makes no mistakes, formed me intentionally just as I am. *God made me deliberately and precisely to be just the person I am for a very specific and holy purpose: to love Him and bring honor to Him with all I am.*

Looking back, I see the painful pressure point of the Academy as an all out effort by God to draw me to Himself. My prideful heart must have needed a bigger two-by-four than the average heart to knock it down to size. But God does not work merely with two-by-fours. Sometimes, He manages to leave His fingerprints on our hearts through sweet, undeserved gifts from His hand.

The Gift of Love

"Three thousand men at the Academy, and you chose me," Mark used to say. I would always remind him that two thousand of those men probably would not even give me the time of day, but I enjoyed it when he marveled anyway. I did the same with him. He was the first man to whom I ever uttered those sacred words, "I love you." I was twenty years old and it seemed I had waited most of my life for him to come along. I had done some dating but had never managed to find a steady boyfriend. But our meeting was not the glamorous "boy meets girl" that I had dreamed of all my life.

We met at the end of our sophomore year. He was interviewing to pick his staff to train the basic cadets when they entered the Academy. I wanted to be a flight sergeant, the one who taught the basics how to march and carry a rifle. I did not know it at the time, but Mark never seriously considered me for the job. He had grown up around the Air Force Academy when it had no women,

7

and Mark believed women had ruined his Air Force Academy. He gave the flight sergeant job to a "more qualified" man, and offered me a paper-pushing job more suitable for a woman.

Had I known this, things might have turned out quite differently. But in my ignorance, I accepted his offer and became his operations sergeant. He never brandished his feelings about women at the Academy, and I managed to fall hard for him before I learned how disparaging those beliefs were. His view of women at the academy seemed to change soon after we met. We were engaged by the fall and since cadets cannot marry, we married the day after graduation. Mark used to say that we did not want to rush into things, so we waited until the day *after* graduation to get married.

He turned out to be a devoted husband. Back then, I thought it was because I had made such a wise choice of a mate, so of course he was a great husband. I know now that life is a series of chances we must choose to take or to let pass by. ***Anytime we enter into a relationship with anyone other than God; there are no guarantees.*** So the ways Mark proved to be a loving husband were a gift straight from God. But even the sweetest gifts from God can be misused.

A Gift Misplaced

My first assignment on active duty in the Air Force was as a civil engineer. Mark finished pilot training to become a flight instructor. Enamored with one another, we spent our first few years as near recluses, except for work. We had been dabbling in faith, but the Throne was occupied with each other. In typical God-style, God applied the pressure on me through my job to get my attention. I was put in charge of the team of civil engineers who was responsible for responding to aircraft accidents to plot parts of aircraft debris and to clean up. I could hear the phone ring in our control center every time there was an aircraft down. I would hold my breath until I heard what type of aircraft it was or until Mark called me.

After a few years of holding my breath, scared, God used my fear to show me the truth: we needed each other more than we needed God. Recognition was the first step toward releasing each other to God. In a deliberate act of obedience, we began reprioritizing. With a concerted effort to seek God both separately and together, we sought God more earnestly in prayer. We prioritized our personal study times over time together. And God, in His unmatched faithfulness, blessed our renewed commitment to Him by bringing us closer to each other as we grew in Him.

More Fingerprints

The fingerprints did not stop there. God maneuvered Mark deliberately to get him in the cockpit of an F-16. Mark had always dreamed of becoming a fighter pilot just like his father. It was his whole reason for attending the Academy. However, while at the Academy, his eyes had deteriorated until he needed a Superintendent's waiver to go to pilot training. Then, because of the waiver, he was only allowed to fly heavy aircraft. So he stayed on after pilot training to become an instructor pilot in the fastest jet he knew he'd ever fly. But God had other plans. After a year as an instructor pilot, the restriction on Mark because of his eyes was lifted. And God plopped him in his dream aircraft, the F-16. It was

9

clear God had us in the F-16 world for a reason, and we were on an adventure to see what it was.

More Humble Pie

Meanwhile, God decided it was time to give me my next lesson in humility. This one was even better than the first. I think God must have smiled knowingly when I declared confidently that I was ready to be a mother. Who is ever really ready to be a mother? But ready or not, God blessed us with a son we named Bryan and soon after, I separated from the Air Force in order to stay home with him. That may sound like a reasonable thing to do. But for the woman who had aspired to follow her Dad to the rank of colonel, it was a huge mental adjustment.

No one was there writing glowing performance reports about how well I had mastered the art of wiping my son's backside. Bryan did not seem impressed with my mothering expertise. No, once again, I had to relearn that my significance came not from what I was doing, but from whose daughter I was. I did not feel much like a princess, but I knew my Daddy was the King. After years of co-existing with God, my new status in life led me to form a real, daily relationship with Him. For the first time, I felt as if God did not need to grab my arm like a parent to get me where He wanted me to go. I reached out for God's hand willingly to follow Him. Humbled again, I was surprised to find that God knew more than I did.

Preparation

Mark's first assignment in the F-16 was to Germany. David was born soon after we arrived. It would have been a picture-perfect assignment for our budding little family, except that Mark was gone for half of it. No sooner had we arrived in a foreign land and had a new baby when Mark was sent off on one of many temporary duties to other countries. Looking back, I can see God was preparing me for single parenthood. By now, I was starting to understand something about God: *He does not answer every prayer as I pray it because if He did, I would never grow.* If God let me decide, I would pray every bump in the road away. But God loves me enough to make me endure the bumps so I can learn to depend on Him and get my focus off myself. After three years in Germany, God sent us to Aviano Airbase, Italy, to stand up a new squadron. Little did I know that the majority of the road before me was full of potholes.

Tutoring Trials

The military wife knows how to move. We are often left to move by ourselves as our husbands fly off to their next assignment. We can throw a household together, get our drapes up and get acquainted with the local area before most are able to get the boxes inside. It is a survival technique; if we did not hurry, we would be moving again before the boxes were unpacked. So it was no big thing that, when we moved to Italy, Mark left me home with three children, four-years-old and under to unpack while he worked twelve hour days. Christina, the newest member of the family turned one just after our arrival. After pulling a month of late nights to put the house together, it was all undone.

Lightning struck a wire outside of our home late at night and shut the power off. The boys' bedroom was in the basement. Mark decided to go look at the fuse box to see if the lightning had blown a fuse. When he arrived in the basement, he knew something was wrong. He found a layer of smoke already a foot deep on the ceiling. Making his way through the smoke toward the fuse box, he found a raging fire. He yelled for my help and we grabbed the children and ran out into the thunderstorm.

Three months and thirteen thousand dollars worth of insurance claims later, we finally recovered from the fire and smoke residual that infiltrated most of the house. But I had been pushed there for a reason. How else could I have grasped the fleeting nature of all the "stuff" we spend so much time accumulating? Had Mark and I been asleep, the boys might have been overcome by smoke before we even knew there was a problem. God's fingerprints were all over the precious lesson this stay-at-home mom learned through the fire: *Life is short; tomorrow there may be no loved ones to care for.*

I should have known that God would see so much room for growth in me that I could expect more "pressure points" to come. Unaware that God's renovation project on my heart had merely just begun, we began planning a family ski trip to Austria. It was almost preempted, however, by an injury to Christina. While protecting his little sister from the "bad guys," one of the boys slammed a door on her finger, partially amputating it. The Italian doctors were able to reattach it, and there is only a small scar remaining today. Although I had been standing right next to Christina, it happened so quickly that there was nothing I could do. This pressure point dramatically illustrated to me the fragility of the human body and reemphasized my inability to control everything. Little by little God was asking me to release all I loved to Him.

With Christina's finger bandaged the size of a lightbulb, we did eventually go on that family ski trip with several other families with small children. While up in Austria, the mothers took an afternoon to escape and tour a famous coat factory to look for bargains. I was looking specifically for a formal winter coat, since mine had been ruined in the fire and we had insurance money to replace it. As we left the mountain, I dragged Mark by the coat outlet to show him a coat I thought would work. He was not crazy about the coat I had picked out, but rather, he liked a casual blazer he saw on a mannequin. He wanted to buy that for me. The blazer was beautiful, but it was quite expensive, and I knew that it would not function as a coat for church and formal functions. I eventually let him buy the blazer for me, but instead of delight, I wore the face of a woman in deep agony, unsure that we had been wise in our purchase. Mark and I were enough alike that we rarely had major disagreements. But Mark was quite perplexed as to how the woman for whom he had just bought an expensive, handsome blazer could be so sullen, and apparently ungrateful.

Even Bryan got into the act as he asked, confused, "Mommy, how come you don't like the coat Dad bought for you?" I explained to them both that it was not so much an issue of gratefulness as it was stewardship. That did not help much. The result of our misunderstanding was about a half-hour of silence in the car ride home. But it was a productive half-hour for me. Once I got over my self-righteous indignation, I began reflecting on my life with Mark. I realized, as I pondered the nature of our disagreement, what a selfless, giving heart he had and how deeply I loved him. I eventually broke the silence by meekly thanking him for the beautiful blazer he had picked out and bought for me. Then, I sincerely apologized for hurting his feelings.

I went on to tell him how when I was a teenager, I used to dream of love and what being in love would be like. I dreamed of the knight in shining armor sweeping me off my feet and gazing deeply in my eyes, blazon with love. But that was as far as I knew to dream. I had no idea how to dream of a love that can develop through years of steadfast commitment, working through tough times together and honoring and cherishing one another despite our faults. "This love is far better than the dream," I whispered to him. Some of God's fingerprints, like this one, reflect His tender, loving heart.

More Trials

After the ski trip things had just begun to get back to "normal" when each of the children, consecutively contracted the stomach flu. Bryan gave it to Christina, and I took Christina to the hospital, concerned that she was becoming dehydrated. I made it back just in time to change my clothes and rattle off directions to Mark for making sloppy joes while I was attending a baby shower. That night, after I came home from the shower, David came down with the flu and began vomiting about the time we were going to bed. Being a third time mom, I had contrived a method of controlling my children's nighttime flu effects to minimize the interruption to the entire household's sleep patterns. I would bring the child to bed with me, and when I heard his stomach gurgling, I would stick his head in a bucket over the edge of the bed. After a quick swab with a wet wipe, we were all able then to resume sleeping with no clean up until morning.

14

Since David had spent the night in our bed, Mark showered at about 4:30 am and dressed in the bathroom, so as not to wake David. Normally, he would have come in after his shower to dress in our room, and I would have had the opportunity to make lewd comments while peeking out from under the covers. But, this time, he tip-toed in and asked me how I felt. After hearing that my stomach was feeling unsettled, he told me not to get up with him, but just to stay in bed and rest. He ate a bowl of cereal while he spent time reading his Bible, as he did every morning. Then, he kissed me good-bye and off he went, as he had done hundreds of times before on early morning training missions. The familiar fragrance of his after-shave lingered in the room after I heard him drive away and comforted me as I drifted off to sleep.

Uninvited Guests

Staring at the coffee pot later that morning while trying to decide whether I was too sick for my morning cup of coffee, I noticed Mark's thoughtful job of cleaning up after himself in the kitchen. Looking closer, I saw a small spot on the countertop made by setting down the sloppy joe spoon. "Why," I half giggled to myself, "can't men see the spoon marks on the counter?" It was then that the doorbell rang. "Oh no," I thought to myself, "I look awful." It was about 10:00 in the morning, and I had been feeling so bad that I had just made it out of the shower, but I had not been able to muster the strength to "fix myself." "Who could it be?" I wondered, not expecting any guests that morning.

Instead of answering the door, I peeked out the front curtain to see who was surprising me. What I saw is a picture that will be ingrained in my memory forever.

There were at least five dark blue Air Force vans parked out front, and I could see several colonels walking up the front path in their service dress uniforms. Every pilot's wife knows what this means, for the Air Force never notifies a family of a loved one's death over the phone.

The Handiwork of God

By God's creative hand
   He was formed
From God's gracious hand
   He was given.
To God's protective hand
   He has returned.
His life was a loving touch
   From the hand of God.

     October 2000

17

A Widow's Lamentation

I've lost him
> And I'm not even sure how it happened.
I began loving my husband
> The first day our eyes met.
He was a joy
> Loving eyes, sweet smile, precious laugh.
But he's gone
> My love couldn't stop the life from leaving his body.

Where do I go?
> How do I heal from the death I died with him?
I can't run far enough
> There is no place the pain is not.
It's the simple things
> That remind me of him and how much I've lost.
The ache is so deep
> It wells up in my soul and crowds out all reason.

I seek You, Lord
> From the depths of my despair and uncertainty.
Are You there?
> Do You really care about my pain?
Do You know
> Just how alone I feel without him?
I cry out in desperation
> Unsure that even You have answers that will satisfy me.

Then You come
> *Reminding me that you watched your son die.*

You cry my tears
> *Understanding how unfair youthful death seems.*

You take my hand
> *And show me things I could not see from down here.*

You hold me close
> *And reassure me of Your love for me.*

I may never get it
> *Exactly what Your plan was when You took him home.*

And the pain remains
> *For you made my wife's heart to beat with my husband's.*

But You show me
> *How even the pain can remind me of Your bigger plan.*

And I finally rest
> *As I let You be God, even the God of my husband's death.*

May 1999

Chapter 2

Hard Pressed:
God Amidst the Turmoil

"We are hard pressed on every side, but not crushed; perplexed, but not in despair; persecuted, but not abandoned; struck down but not destroyed."   II Corinthians 4:8-9

The doorbell rang again. I stood, frozen, in the living room. My heart and mind were racing. I considered not answering the door, pretending I was not there, but I knew I could not do that. I took a deep breath, as if it were going to be the last chance I would have to breathe real oxygen. Then I forced myself to walk, mechanically, to the door, open it and enter one of my worst nightmares.

At the door stood two of our good friends, Mark's squadron commander, Gary and his wife, Colette. Tears were streaming down both their faces. "Hi, Patti," Gary braved, "There's been an accident." Gary and Colette had been stationed with us in Germany, and we had spent many days studying God's Word together. I trusted them both implicitly. Yet at that moment, I wanted them both to be despicable liars, contriving a horribly wicked practical joke. The pain and compassion in their eyes told me such was not the case. One of the colonel's wives asked if she could take the children to another room. "No," I am sure I snapped at her, "we do things as a family." I somehow invited them all in the living room where I heard what little the Air Force knew at that time.

Mark had gone out in his single seat fighter with two other jets on a training mission over the Adriatic Sea. It was a beautiful day, not a cloud in sight. During the first maneuver of the morning, Mark had broken hard left, and his wingman and the "enemy" plane had gone right, each trying to out-maneuver the other to "kill" the "enemy". The last words they heard from Mark were his instruction to his wingman to continue the fight, "Bane Two, *press*." As the other two continued their "dog fight" they soon realized that Mark was not returning radio calls. They knocked off the fight and circling around saw only a puff of smoke in the air and a ring of oil in the water. Search and recovery crews were on their way to the site, but it did not look as if Mark had bailed out.

A Transforming Moment

After hearing the full story, I had no idea what to do. I wanted to run as fast as my legs would carry me, until the pain in my legs and lungs was greater than the pain in my heart. I wanted to hide my head under a pillow and sleep until the nightmare passed. But I knew there was no place I could escape from the truth. *So I did what I had always hoped I would do if this situation ever arrived.* I watched myself gather my little children around me: Bryan, a week shy of five years old, David, three years old, and Christina, who as just one and one-half years old.

I got down on my knees and holding the children tightly, I prayed for Mark, if there were a chance he was alive, that God would bring him home safely. But if we had already lost him, as it appeared, I thanked God for ten wonderful years with him as my husband. I thanked God for the gift of having had such a wonderful man as the loving father of my children. In that moment, I watched myself become, if even for an instant, the woman I knew God wanted me to be.

Bryan was the only one of the children who could understand what was going on. For the next half-hour he sat on Colette's lap and cried. I think she needed to hold him as much as he needed to be held. The younger two just hated to see their Mommy cry, so they each hugged me warmly before running off to play.

A Long Night

The sun went down much too quickly that night as I knew Mark's chances of surviving the crash and enduring a night in the frigid waters of the Adriatic Sea in January were almost none. In my heart, I knew he had died. Radio calls were as second nature to him from his nine and one-half years of flying as was walking. The times I had been allowed to taxi a jet with him, I had been entranced with his comfort level in the jet; it was merely an extension of himself. So I knew that, if Mark did not make any radio calls, it was because he could not. His last radio call echoed in my head, while my mind raced wildly to make sense of his last word, "**Press**." What was he saying to me? What was God telling me?

That night, I lay in bed, sleepless, thinking of all these things. The tears seemed to have an endless supply as they continually ran down my cheeks and into my ears. At one point I got up and put tissues in my ears to prevent them from filling up with salt water. Tissue after tissue, the night crept on.

No one had ever told me that emotional pain could hurt much deeper than physical pain. I had birthed three children naturally and thought I knew what pain was. But this pain felt like a gaping, sucking chest wound. It literally felt as if half of my heart had been ripped away. It was a pain I was to learn to live with for months,

23

sometimes subsiding long enough for exhaustion to give way to periods of sleep, only to be startled awake by the ache and another adrenaline surge a few minutes later. The wound made me want to walk hunched over, to protect it. I found myself surprised when I ran across someone who did not notice my wound because it engulfed me so, I thought it might swallow me up.

A Meeting with God

The morning brought no new hope for Mark's survival. I decided I needed to go for a run just to get out of the house. I knew I needed an extra dose of lucidity that morning. Well meaning, caring folks swarmed all over the house, but I needed to find God and meet with Him face to face. Off I went, running much too fast at first, through the streets of our little Italian village, longing for the seclusion of the dirt road at the end of the village. I soon discovered that the combination of crying and sprinting produces hyperventilation, as well as making a spectacle for the Italian pedestrians to enjoy.

I was forced to slow my pace and soon I was alone with God. In desperation, I cried out to the God I love, "Lord, I am hurting deeply and feel so confused. I do not understand why you have taken my godly husband and the father of my children. I believe you know what you are doing, but for my weak, human flesh, could you just give me a glimpse of the bigger picture You see? I need that so desperately right now, so that I can rest in the perfection of Your ways." Then I tried to just listen, to clear my mind of the myriad of thoughts swirling around threatening to undo me.

I focused on God, Himself, as best as my unfocused mind could do. Then, to my amazement, I began to see clearly a small portion of God's omniscient plan. There was no thundering voice from heaven, but I knew that this was bigger than Mark, and bigger than our children and bigger than my pain. This was about God bringing home one of His own, so He could draw more people to Himself. We had known that God was at work in a mighty way in Aviano, the Air Base to which we were assigned. Now, He wanted to continue that work through Mark's death and memorial service. I knew then, that the priority of the service had to be first to honor God. I knew Mark would have wanted it that way, too.

As I began to feel some excitement at the eternal plan God was making clear in my mind, He dropped a bomb on me which only God could pull off. God was inviting me to be a part of His mighty plan. I began sensing that God wanted me to speak at the memorial service. "But God," I argued out loud, "the widow does not speak at these things. She just sits in the front row and cries!" There was, again, no audible response, but I sensed God's patience and sense of humor as He put me in my place, again, "Who makes the rules, Patti?"

God had been doing this kind of thing for several years now. Ever since I began to get deeply into His Word and to know Him, He would bring to mind truths from His word and they would convict me on the spot. I desperately wanted to hear the Holy Spirit's voice but I did not always like what He said. When He spoke, it usually meant there was an area of my life that needed cleaning up. This time he seemed to be screaming at me, "Believe me, Patti!" He was prompting me to step out on faith, to see for myself that He was real.

But I was not finished with God yet. "God I see how you are taking care of the unsaved at Aviano Air

Base, allowing them to hear about You at the service, but what about our children, are their souls important to You too? How can I rear them to know You without their godly father?" God brought to mind the many scriptures where He has said He will be Father to the fatherless. I knew then that it would be my job to point them to their perfect Father, the one who loves them more than Mark ever possibly could. And I needed to trust God's nature, knowing that He would not have taken Mark home if doing so were going to decrease my children's opportunity to know Him.

God was asking me to believe that He was able actually to increase their exposure to Himself through Mark's death. I had no idea how God was going to do this, but I chose to trust my God who had proven Himself trustworthy. Although I find myself still playing a constant game of tug of war with God over my children, I know that He is the greatest lover of my children's hearts and souls. They are safe with Him.

It Is Finished

It was Saturday, about 48 hours after Mark's crash when General Michael Ryan came to my home on an official visit. It was his responsibility to make the decision when Mark would be officially declared dead. By this time, my in-laws had arrived from their home in Colorado Springs and were there at my side. General Ryan logically and methodically laid out all the facts he had considered in making his decision: the eye witness accounts from the pilots flying with Mark; the undeployed chute; the unused life raft; no ships in the vicinity at the time of the crash; and the search and rescue crew's inability to locate Mark.

He did not tell me anything I did not already know, but it seemed so final to hear him make a legal declaration of Mark's death. In a numb, robotic manner, I asked questions, only because I felt as if I should not accept this verdict unless I, too, were convinced. General Ryan answered my questions patiently, then stepped out of his official capacity and spoke to us as friends. He had lost a brother flying a fighter over the ocean during the Vietnam War. General Ryan's loving concern and empathy turned what could have seemed like a cold, unfeeling visit into a hug from a friend who understood our pain. When the official meeting was finally over, and General Ryan left, I had a new identity. I was no longer Mark's wife; I was his widow.

Facing an Unthinkable Task

It was time to face the hardest thing I could ever imagine doing: telling my children that their Daddy was dead. I took Bryan in the bathroom where we could have privacy and I told him. Bryan held onto me and sobbed. As I held his thin little heaving body, I felt as if my own heart too would burst out of my body. The pain of seeing my child's grief was much harder to bear than my own. I could not make it better; I could not kiss this one away. We both cried until no more tears came.

I gathered myself and went to find his brother. I anticipated a similar response as I brought David into the bathroom. He had always been so close to his father. He is a real guy's guy, and had an insatiable appetite for being with his Daddy. After carefully, agonizingly describing his father's death in words I thought a three-year-old little boy could digest, I looked, tearfully into my son's piercingly bright blue eyes, expecting the worst. He

27

paused for a moment, as if absorbing it all, then said, innocently, "Mommy, can I watch a movie now?" "Yes, sweetheart," I was able to reply calmly. But inside, I was screaming out, confused by his response.

I knew God had his protective hand over David's heart, preventing him from fully grasping what I was saying to him. I knew his young emotions could not handle such grief, and that this must be God's way of showing His gentle, loving care for David. But at the same time, I wanted to grab David and shake him and shout loudly in his face, "Don't you understand what you've lost?" At that moment, my emotions and thoughts seemed as erratic as they had ever been, a frame of mind that became the norm over many months to come.

I have always been a logical person, so when I felt such wild, irrational and rapid mood swings, it scared me. I sat in the bathroom and sobbed. With outstretched hands, I presented God with my gnarled, raw, festering emotions. I didn't know what to do with them and I hoped God would. There in the bathroom, I came before the throne of God. And God calmed the storm. He showed me that I needed to slow down, and not to rely on my first reactions. He made it clear that I would need to ask for help, something my proud heart resists, but my children's and my well being depended on it. This was my first of many lessons in handling shock and grief.

There was no need to try to tell a one-year-old that her father had died. Christina continued to wander around our villa on her fledgling legs, as joyful as ever. That night and many nights after, I cried all the way through "Jesus Loves Me" as I sang and rocked her before laying her down to sleep. I pictured Mark holding her and singing off-key as he did most nights, and it broke my heart to realize that she would never be held or sung to by her father again.

Unwanted Decisions

The next few days were filled with a barrage of endless legal matters and big decisions. It seemed as if every person on base were required to brief me on something. At times I wanted to run and hide, screaming, "I don't care, leave me alone." But I knew each of these experts truly wanted to help me so I tried to be patient. Some decisions seemed annoyingly inappropriate for the context.

When faced with decisions of what to do with insurance money, it made me sick to my stomach to think that I would be paid money because of Mark's death. I did not want money; I wanted Mark. I wanted it all to go away. My son, Bryan expressed the same sentiment when one night, as I was putting him to bed he said, "Mommy, I want all those people to go away and I want Daddy to come home." But Mark did not come home, a fact that none of us would fully comprehend until the days turned into weeks, the weeks to months and the months to years.

I have never been one to shy away from making big decisions, but all that I faced these first few days was too much for me to comprehend. With the help of my father-in-law, a retired four star general, I made as many decisions as possible, knowing that many companies pay him big bucks for his advice and I was getting it for free. I had all of Aviano Air Base at my beck and call, anxious to help, and I feared any decision made later would result in much more work for everyone. Looking back, my actions seem cold, unfeeling, and almost mercenary. But I wonder if part of God's plan for a widow's survival is to load her with busy-work in the early months so she has a chance to work through the initial acceptance of the death in small bits and pieces. If we all could go off in our own rooms and work through our grief immediately, I wonder how many widows would ever emerge.

A Safe Harbor

There were times when I needed to assimilate some of the impact of Mark's death in my life. I would escape to the solitude of the basement, and in Mark's office I would work on planning the memorial service. I felt such a peace each time I thought of God's eternal perspective. I knew it was an honor that God wanted to use me to bring Him glory. Like a child who desperately wants to please a parent, so I wanted to be faithful to what God had laid on my heart for the people of Aviano. This was therapy that no psychologist could have employed effectively. In the midst of my pain, God showed me how to care for the souls of others, to move out of myself so I could minister to those who wanted to minister to me.

Many of those who would come to the memorial service had grown up attending churches with plenty of religious and ceremonial fanfare but had missed the heart of God. I wanted none of that in this service. I wanted God, in His purest form to be seen and felt. While retaining the military ceremony, I threw out all the religious and military protocol. Nothing would be said about God in flowery language or ritualistic phrases, which often allow us to appease our desire to feel as if we are doing something spiritual, but which actually prevent our minds from being challenged. Even saints with great depth of love for and faith in God, have trouble hearing and comprehending words they have said a thousand times, regardless of the spiritual accuracy and intensity of the words. Everything in Mark's service was to be genuine and conversational.

All this came to me much more clearly than picking the location of the service. I was driven around Aviano AB looking at sites large enough to hold the expected 500+ attendees. None seemed to suit, until we drove out on the flight line. There, with the smell of the jet's fuel, JP-4, and the sound of jet engines roaring, I knew we were, at last, where we needed to be. I looked at several possibilities and finally decided to have the service in the hardened aircraft shelter where Mark launched his last flight. I did not have a chance to see the actual shelter until the morning of the service.

Strength from Above

The morning of his memorial service, exactly a week after his crash, the sky was perfectly clear and deep blue like Mark's eyes. I had my scripted talk in hand as we were driven out to the shelter. I had asked the wing commander's wife, Marky Campbell, to read my speech should I be unable to control my sobbing. But as we approached the shelter, I felt a peace and assurance I have never known before. God was there, holding me and smiling. I knew God's strength would be enough. The shelter was pointed directly at an unobstructed view of Piancavallo, the highest peak on the snow-capped range just north of Aviano. To me, the mountains have always been irrefutable evidence of God's power and wisdom:

> *"He made the earth by His power;*
> *He founded the world by His wisdom*

31

Although I was shivering, the radiance of God's presence kept me warm. I was comforted to know that this is the last sight Mark had seen as he was taxiing his jet out for his final sortie. I knew this scene would have caused Mark to pause and pray to the God he loved and was only moments away from seeing face to face. Girded by strength not my own, I shared from my heart with love for the people of Aviano. I finished my part without as much as a whimper. Then I sat and laughed and cried with the slew of speakers to follow, each sharing a unique perspective on Mark's life. And I worshipped in spirit and in truth as I have never worshipped before or since.

Only a few days later my little family and I and our rather large entourage of relatives were on a plane, leaving Italy for good. My memories of that trip are merely a blur. I know it was hard to leave some of my best friends in Aviano. It was obvious that, since they too were pilot's wives, that they would be dreading every flight their husbands would take for quite some time. But once again, God graciously focused my mind on the future, and He gave me an excitement for the things He would do at the funeral at the US Air Force Academy.

A Repeat Performance

Hundreds of friends, family and acquaintances braved blizzard conditions to fill the Academy chapel. Sitting in a front row of the chapel, my mind was racing as I stared at the flag-draped casket placed ceremonially just in front of the steps where Mark and I had cheerfully and naively recited those famous words, "...until death do us part." Never would I have imagined that I would be bringing his remains back to this spot where we had made that commitment to each other. As thoughts of those happy times filled my mind, in stark contrast to the emotions of this day, I realized that our vows had been fulfilled. While the relationship itself had been severed swiftly, we had been given the gift of being one of the couples who had made it; only death had parted us.

Sitting in the chapel of the school Mark had wanted to go to most of his life, I once again felt God's presence in a real way. This time, I had no back-up speaker for myself because I had felt, firsthand, God's power flow through me in Aviano and I was sure He would be there again. I felt so honored to be able to use the platform God had given me, as undesirable as it may have been, to bring Him glory. I may never know if God used that service or the one in Aviano to move in the hearts or lives of any of the attendees there, but I knew the worship experience was some of the sweetest I had ever known. And I knew that I had been faithful to do the part He had asked me to do.

Desperately Seeking Comfort

Taken home so young, without explanation.
    Life cut short in an instant.
    And life for those left, never the same.
So much potential, never realized.
    So many things, unsaid.
    So much love, yet to be given.
Photos lack a critical dimension.
    All seem rudely out of focus.
    None satisfy the longing for a touch.
Tears come and go with no distinguishable pattern.
    Some are a welcome relief.
    Some intrude, uninvited.
Memories enmesh with dreams.
    Reality seems unreal,
    The truth, a lie.
Time passes without permission.
    Grass grows over the grave far too soon.
    The pain ignores the passing time.
But long nights end in beautiful sunrises.
    And little heads rise all too early, chattering.
    Reminders from God that life goes on, somehow.
Joy is available through the Giver and Taker of life.
    He who comprehends all things has a plan.
    He can be trusted.
Seeking Him is suddenly the only thing that makes sense,
    In a world where confusion seeks to rule,
    Where self-reliance doesn't work.
The Comforter comes in a mighty way,
    To envelop the mourning who seek His face,
    Those waiting for their turn to go home.
And comfort is found in His loving arms.

October 1995

The Identity Search of a Widow

Who am I?
I used to be the wife and helpmate of a wonderful, Godly man.
But now he's gone, for good.
He's in the room Christ prepared for him in heaven.
But I'm still here...without him.
It hurts.
I miss him.
He was my buddy.
I'm tempted to ask God, "Why?"
But I choose to stand firm in my faith.
I choose to become trusting, childlike.
I won't question God's motives, His judgment, His sovereignty or
His love for me.
For I know His ways are not my ways.
And His ways are righteous.
I will trust in His master plan.
I will rest in His loving arms.
I will draw on His strength.
I will lean on His promises.
I won't ask, "Why?"
I will ask expectantly, "How?"
"How will You use his death for Your glory?"
"How can I best serve You through my widowhood?"
"How can I point my children toward You, as their perfect
Father?"
"How can I let go and trust You to meet my every need?"
Moment by moment I will ask, "How?"
And I will wait patiently and silently for His answers with a
thankful heart.
Thankful for the love of a wonderful man; many never
experience such a love.
Thankful for the time I had with him and the way he nurtured
my relationship with God.
Thankful that I have never had to wonder where my best friend
is now.
Thankful that an awesome God would choose me to bear witness
of His strength.
Thankful that God understands my pain and is here to comfort
me.

"My God, I know who You are.
You're the one who brought us together.
You joined the two of us into one.
You know that when my husband died, I became a half.
But through my halfness, Your love makes me whole.
I know who I am.
I am a widow in mourning,
But I am whole.
For I am a beloved child of Yours."

May 1995

Chapter 3

Pressure Cooker:
Big Changes

"By faith Abraham, when called to go to a place he would later receive as his inheritance, obeyed and went, even though he did not know where he was going."   Hebrews 11:8

"Widow," the word even sounds old. Most of the widows I knew were at least in their 60's. All of their children were grown. Only once had I met a widow who was in her 30's with toddlers. Looking back, I never took the time to understand her pain or the significance of her title. But now the title "widow" was mine. Accepting this fact was a slow process but probably among the easiest of the big adjustments I needed to make.

An Erratic Thought Life

Taking charge of my thoughts continued to be a constant struggle. Things ran through my mind which seemed irreverent, unfaithful, disloyal, selfish, frightening and even ridiculous, during those first few days and months after Mark's death, thoughts that I was embarrassed to have, much less share with anyone else. But I found it comforting to know that God knew my thoughts completely:

> *O Lord, You have searched me and you know me.*
> *You know when I sit and when I rise;*
> *You perceive my thoughts form afar.*
> *You discern my going out and my lying down;*
> *You are familiar with all my ways.*

Before a word is on my tongue You know it
completely, O Lord.
Psalm 139:1-4 (NIV)

When you become sure that God knows all your thoughts and motivations, then you have two responses: You can act as if He does not know (He recognizes those thoughts, too) or you can acknowledge His participation in your thoughts. It seemed prudent to me that, if I were having thoughts that made me uncomfortable, then rather than try to ignore or run from them, I ought consciously to give them to the One who understands my thoughts, my motivations, and my discomfort. I often said, "God, You know I just had this thought. I can not hide anything from you. But I do not know why I am having this thought, or what to do with it, so I want to give it to You. Please align my heart with Yours. Help me dwell on only those thoughts You have for me." Some of the thoughts stemmed from my selfish flesh; some were just logical concerns for a woman whose tangible love, security and identity had just been ripped from her. Everything I thought to be true about my future was now in question. So question, I did.

Revised Questioning

During the first few months as I continually grilled God with questions, I found God was big enough to handle my questions, but often my asking would more closely resemble whining. As a parent, I have watched with amusement as my children whine, and I have noticed my reaction to it. When my child whines, his demanding little attitude screams to the world that it should revolve around him. He refuses to see that there could be something bigger and more important involved than his own immediate desires. With this attitude, no reasoning or logical answer is sufficient. He has allowed his own selfish desires to swallow him up. The goal of his whining then is not to seek the true, right or best answers, but to manipulate those with power into giving in to his desires. And, if that is not accomplished, then his whining serves to display his misery and make those around him miserable as well.

My whining was often just like that, a complaint hidden in the form of a question. While God often met me in my whining, gently acknowledging the ways my situation seemed unfair, I soon found the whining I chose to do hurt me and my attitude toward my life. Whenever I approached God in a demanding, accusatory fashion, I showed God and myself with my attitude that I did not really believe God was God. I was not coming to the Creator and Sustainer of this universe respectfully, humbly to ask questions about the situation He had ordained for me and ways He would use me. I was coming to rant and rave at an unfair God who did not know what He was doing or could not be trusted to do what is best in my life and in the lives of those I care about.

Whining to God removed the certainty of God's character and His wisdom from my focus and replaced them with my desires. The result of my whining was that it shook my whole world and stripped me of God's perfect peace and joy. There is comfort and security in the knowledge that, even in the most frightening and confusing times of our lives, that the character and truth of God remain intact. My whining removed that security. Job discovered this truth after he had whined to God (justifiably in our minds!):

"I know that you can do all things;
No plan of yours can be thwarted.
You asked, 'Who is this that obscures my counsel without
   knowledge?'
Surely I spoke of things I did not understand,
Things too wonderful for me to know." Job 42:2-3 (NIV)

Job obviously changed his mode of operation from whining to humbly and honestly approaching the throne with his questions.

I decided I needed to revise the ways I approached God as well. I did not want to be His whining child, flailing about, screaming at him with clenched fists, and insisting that I knew what was best in the bigger picture. Rather, as a minimum, I wanted to try to come to God with my questions in a respectful, submissive manner, keeping in mind to whom I was asking the questions. I tried to begin by praising God, whether I felt like it or not. My praise of God is solely for me. He does not need my praise, He is secure in who He is. I praise Him to help me remember to whom I am speaking and the kind of power He has. I praise Him to remind myself that He is not merely the author of wisdom, but He *is* wisdom. I am surely not able to say I praise Him as much as I should, but I know it is what is best for me as well as what will allow me to be open to God's wisdom:

"If any of you lacks wisdom, he should ask God, who gives generously to all without finding fault, and it will be given to him."   *James 1:5 (NIV)*

So who needs wisdom? I know I need it, so I should be asking God for it in any and every situation. Sometimes, even with these truths firmly in my mind, I

40

still whine to God. Sometimes, I do not even want to know the answers to my questions; I just want to cry on God's shoulder. God has always been patient and has let me do just that, but, when I am finally ready to listen and seek God's wisdom, He is faithful to point me toward His truths. He has always been there tenderly guiding me in the midst of the big confusing adjustments that enveloped me. Sometimes, His wisdom comes through His Word, sometimes through nature, sometimes through faithful friends who do not just commiserate with me but who are courageous enough to point me to God's truths even when I do not want to hear them. Once, it came through a memory I could not shake.

Filling the Heart Hole

Only days before Mark's death, I remember being held tightly by Mark in the night and whispering to him, "What would I do without you?" He responded with the same sweet words, "What would I do without *you*?" which reflected our mutual longings to live out the remainder of our lives together. Now, rather than posing this poignant rhetorical question as a way to reassure Mark that he was irreplaceable in my life, it was, ironically, a question which had to be candidly addressed, because it was my unmistakable future. What *would* I do?

The answer was clear, although not comforting. I would miss Mark terribly minute by minute. I would mourn and grieve, not for Mark's status, but for the husband I had lost and the father my children had lost. I *knew* Mark was in a better place, and he had the advantage of seeing that bigger picture God could see. But I was stuck down here without him, missing his help and his guidance, but mostly just missing his presence. Any chore

41

was bearable and even fun with him at my side. I would have rather spent time with him than anyone else in the whole world. When I was not with him, I knew he would care about what I had done without him, and it would make those tasks bearable, too.

The emptiness was much greater than the void left when he had to leave on deployments, for then I knew he might be thousands of miles away, but he was still caring about me and wanting to hear about even the smallest details of our lives. When he died, what I missed the most was the emotional anchoring I felt from a man who knew me better than anyone else did and loved me anyway. For years after Mark's death, I subconsciously expected him to walk through the door, so I could share with him the details of my struggles and my victories since his death. We had shared so much for so long, that it was a huge and painfully slow adjustment before my desire for an intimate relationship could be satisfied not by my visible, affectionate, fleshly husband but by a God I could not see or touch. That was one of the hardest but the most worthwhile adjustments I have ever had to make.

Finding New Dreams

Mark and I had spoken often in jest, but with sincerity, of how we planned to some day have pink and blue Efferdent cups to prevent the embarrassment of getting our dentures mixed up at night. I was faced with not just missing Mark in my day to day life, but missing Mark in my dreams of the future. Any time I saw elderly couples gently helping each other walk, or heard of a 50th wedding anniversary, the ache in my soul was almost debilitating. I had to begin to construct new dreams of my future life, without Mark or any man. I knew only God could fill the void left by Mark in my life in a healthy manner. I knew I would have to learn how to relish the joy of God's presence in my life and to count on His presence alone as I dreamed of the future.

One might think that for a widow who truly loved her husband that it might be months or even years before she would allow herself to entertain thoughts about dating and remarriage. For me it was days. I loved being married so much. I enjoyed the warmth and security of caring for someone who cared equally about me. I relished the romance in my marriage. I treasured any time I spent with my man, my lover and my best friend. I knew I would not want to live out the rest of my days alone, so I hoped that God might someday allow me to remarry. Not every widow allows herself these thoughts as soon as I did, nor would she admit it if she had. However, I have come to believe that desiring marriage again reflects on the health of the lost marriage and gives a widow's mind something about which she can dream. A mind focused on what is lost is much more likely to experience discouragement and hopelessness than one focused on the joys ahead God is able to provide.

Becoming Single Again

I would like to say my first fears of dating and remarriage were for my three children, but they were not. My "profoundly spiritual mind" turned at once to fears about my own body. It had gone through three pregnancies, three births and three years of nursing. These events, combined with age and gravity, had taken their toll on my body, and it no longer looked as it did when I was 18. I had always been confident when I was with Mark, partly because of his reassurances, but mostly because he

43

had been with me through all those events and had loved and appreciated my body and what it had become. Marriage to any one else was quite a frightening prospect.

The fact that I was even pondering this image led me to another set of uncomfortable questions. What did it mean that I was even thinking of ever being with another man? Was I being unfaithful just to have those thoughts? Thus began my long, slow, confusing journey from being married to being single. While technically speaking, it had happened in an instant, I spent ten years of my life devoting myself to fidelity with one man. So while my mind skipped on ahead to dream of and hope for a new relationship some day, my heart was still married to Mark and would be for some time.

My thoughts eventually did turn outward enough for me to wonder how remarriage might affect my children. If I were to remarry, could anyone love my children as Mark did? Should I surgically remove the option of again becoming pregnant to protect my children from facing any possibility of being the less-loved stepchildren? Would the benefits of having a new man in our home outweigh the painful adjustments, which would seem inevitable for any blended family, no matter how tremendous the blend?

I knew many of these thoughts could turn into anxieties, then worries and even obsessions if I were to allow them to fester. During this time, especially, there was always the temptation to stew, and work myself up into a frazzled mess over these questions. But I knew my future and every detail therein was in God's hands, whether I chose to acknowledge that or not. I knew God had given me the free will to acknowledge His sovereignty in each of those areas, and to rest in His plan for my life. I would like to say I figured this out and gave it to God and

44

that was the last of my anxieties. But the truth is these worries arose over and over in my mind.

So, I had to make a moment by moment choice not to take these matters into my own hands. I constantly had to remind myself that I am physically, as I am, because that is how God designed me. To tamper with that out of fear would be disrespectful to my creator. I knew that the quality of a man who would interest me some day would be one who loved God first. He would be trustworthy with my physical flaws and the hearts and souls of my children. As I replayed these truths over and over in my mind, my anxieties about what might lie ahead decreased. I deliberately put these thoughts and questions into God's reassuring hands, and the temptation to build high protective walls around my children and myself became unnecessary. God would be the protector of our hearts and souls when dating and remarriage became a possibility.

Revised Questioning...Again

Although I daydreamed of marriage again, God knows that my desire to move backward in time rather than forward was obvious. It was evidenced by the questions I continued to pose to God: "God, Mark was so wonderful. He was such a caring, fun father to the children. He was kind, attentive and loving toward me. And he was smart, skilled, and handsome. You could never bring me another man as wonderful as Mark with whom I could share the kind of love we had." Sometimes when my children approach me this way, I let it be as they say, since they know so much. God would have been quite justified in saying, "OK, since you know more than I do, I

45

will let you have your way. You are right, I can not give you another gift like the one that you had in Mark."

But God was merciful to me and instead chose to remind me to whom I was talking. Once again, there was no audible message, but in my spirit, I heard a resounding, "Excuse me? What is it that I can not do?" Undoubtedly, it had been God who had brought Mark to me, and He was perfectly capable of bringing me someone else whom I could love and enjoy as I enjoyed Mark. As I began writing this, I did not know if God had it in His mighty plan to bless me in that way. But I never doubted that He was able.

New Existential Fears

Having lost Mark, fears for my children's lives and my own life inevitably began to encircle me. I began questioning God and the ways in which He cares for us.

"Consider how the lilies grow. They do not labor or spin. Yet I tell you, not even Solomon in all his splendor was dressed like one of these. If that is how God clothes the grass of the field, which is here today and tomorrow is thrown into the fire, how much more will he clothe you, O you of little faith?"
Luke 12:27-28 (NIV)

I pondered this promise of God's care and I thought of Mark's body. "Didn't you care as much for Mark's body as you do for the lilies of the field which you clothe and care for so beautifully?" It was hard to imagine how God had kept this promise. But He knew this time I was sincerely and earnestly seeking His truths, and He set them before me in the form of some verses. The first are the words given by the angels when the women arrived

46

and found the tomb where Jesus had been laid to be empty:

"They found the stone rolled away from the tomb, but when they entered, they did not find the body of the Lord Jesus. While they were wondering about this, suddenly two men in clothes that gleamed like lightning stood beside them. In their fright, the women bowed down with their faces to the ground, but the men said to them, "Why do you look for the living among the dead?"
Luke 24:2-5 (NIV)

God showed me through these verses that I had been looking for Mark in the wrong place. He was not in the body, which had been scattered across the Adriatic Sea. I was looking for the living, Mark's soul, among the dead, his body. Mark had been cared for just as God had said. God shook the stick in the jet, indicating that He had taken control of the plane, and flew Mark's spirit up to heaven where he was being cared for eternally. There was a second verse of reassurance from God:

"Do not be afraid of those who kill the body but cannot kill the soul. Rather, be afraid of the One who can destroy both soul and body in hell. Are not two sparrows sold for a penny? Yet not one of them will fall to the ground apart from the will of your Father."
Matthew 10: 28-29 (NIV)

Many well-meaning Christians tried to reassure me that this was not God's plan, that God wanted to care for Mark, but in a fallen sinful world, Satan loves to use his powers to destroy God's people. Well, I do not doubt that Satan would love to destroy God's people, but the truth is that God is the ruler of this universe, not Satan. Satan probably thought he had won a grand victory when Mark

47

died and one of the lights in the dark fighter pilot world went out, but it was in God's plan. God, the Omniscient One, knew ahead of time how He would take one of His own home and in doing so would multiply His light.

"I tell you the truth, unless a kernel of wheat falls to the ground and dies, it remains only a single seed. But if it dies, it produces many seeds."   John 12:24 (NIV)

God, not Satan, allowed Mark to die so that many seeds would be produced for Him. And God cared for Mark's soul in heaven as He promised He would. While I felt reassured by the answers God had given me, it took a while for me to transfer them into reassurances about my own life and my children's lives.

Contemplating My Mortality

Making up a revised will after Mark died was among the high priority tasks I needed to accomplish. But carrying out this chore did not relieve me of my anxieties about my own death. I battled not with fears of dying myself, but with concerns for my children. Nightmare after nightmare left me begging God to let me stay on the earth longer to care for my children. Then one night after such an episode, I forced myself to face my worst fears. So what would happen if I were to die? Would it be hard on my children? Yes. Would God still be their God, and would He be able to care for them without me? Yes. I had to come to grips with my own expendability in God's sovereign plan so that my own fears would not cripple me.

My mission had to be to relax and let God be in charge (since He was anyway) and do the best job of mothering my children while God kept me in that position.

What freedom there was in realizing that God is as sufficient for my children as He is for me, and He loves them immeasurably more than I do anyway. But there were the also pragmatic as well as spiritual concerns about parenting without a man around.

Becoming a Single Mother

My mother-in-law was the tool God used to teach me one of the most valuable practical lessons I was to learn. I was sharing with her how I was trying to figure out how to be father and mother to the children. Mom, an Air Force wife for 35 years and mother of five children, had spent many months and years separated from her husband and the children's father. Her advice? "Do not try to be mother and father." She found freedom in just resolving to be the best mother she could be. She could not be both mother and father to the children, and it was confusing to them when she tried. What freedom rang with those words. I had always wanted to be the best mother I could be and that was one thing in my life that did not have to change, thank God. But what did change was that I had to make an extra effort to be sure that there were men in my children's life who cared for them and taught them some of the things a man ought to teach them. But there were more practical adjustments yet to be made.

I found it was hard to tell people I was a single mother. The story was too long to go into with strangers. One suggestion made to me was that I ought to figure out a concise way of letting people know how I had become a single mother, so they would not think it was through divorce or promiscuity. One morning on one of my long runs, I was pondering ways to do just that, when God graciously intervened. I felt the disciplining hand of God

49

sweep over me. "Are you doing this because you think you are better than my daughters who are single mothers through divorce or promiscuity? How will you be able to minister to my hurting daughters from atop your pedestal?"

When God puts conviction in a heart there is no mistaking it. I have seen vividly that, once again, God knew what He was talking about. The never married and divorced mothers I have met are some of the most hurting people with whom I have come in contact. The path God chose to make me a single mother, although hard, was a gift. I did not have to deal with the anguish, the guilt, the rejection, or the betrayal that so many of them faced. Mark died loving me, and wanting to be there with and for the children and me. But mostly, I am thankful that I did not lose my first love, and I never will. I can not imagine going through what some of these single mothers have gone through without knowing God's loving tender, sovereign hand was holding mine. If I considered myself better than any of those fellow single mothers, there is no way God could have used me to come alongside them and minister to any of them.

Moving a Life

The unwanted emotional adjustments would have been plenty to deal with at the time, but the logistical adjustments hit at the same time. Yet, looking back, I can see the hand of God moving in practical ways to care for this widow. I knew I could not remain in Italy for long, that I needed to and wanted to move back the United States, soon. So in the first few days following Mark's death, I made the decision to relocate to Colorado Springs. Since I was taking the children across the Atlantic for the funeral, it did not make sense to me to drag them all the way back to Italy to pack out our house. Some precious God-given friends took over all the legal and logistical arrangements remaining for us there in Italy.

Meanwhile, I had moved in temporarily with my parents in Virginia for a time of healing. My mother had been a schoolteacher for 20-1/2 years in the high school I had attended. Seventeen days before Mark's crash, my mother knew in her heart that it was time to retire. She surprised everyone with the news and was allowed to retire in the middle of the school year rather than a normal summer retirement. A woman with an incredible servant's heart, God prompted Mom to make herself available to meet my needs with her willing and able help, as only my Mom could have done. I had time to write out things about Mark and his death that I knew I wanted always to remember and to share with my children. She cared for my children and added stability to their lives as I laid all my intensely painful emotions at God's feet and allowed Him to begin the healing work in my heart. Soon, however, I began feeling an intense desire to set up my own home with my children and begin rebuilding our lives together.

April fools day I flew from Virginia to Colorado with the children to begin my search for a home. A hunt and a decision which Mark and I would have thoroughly enjoyed doing together was now a lonely burdensome chore. But God's hand moved clearly and swiftly. It was as if God had seen His child suffer enough and He now wanted to show me His sweet provision. I signed a contract on the 10th of April, my 32nd birthday. Although my in-laws, James and Alice McCarthy lived in Colorado, I would have moved there even if they were not there. I knew I needed quickly to find solid Christian friends and a

51

church family and was sure I would find both easily there. However, beside Himself, God knew what it was that I needed most.

Mom McCarthy had become more than a mother-in-law to me when we both were stationed in Germany, and Mark was deployed half of our three-year tour there. I spent many holidays and long stretches of time with Mark's parents in their Stuttgart home. I think it was heart-warming for Mark to discover that his mother and I had become such close friends during his absence, but he had no way of knowing how critical that relationship was to become to us both. I know our coming to Colorado was a boost for Mom McCarthy's emotional state, as it helped her focus on ways to help us through that hard time. It was and still is a joy for her to spend time and contribute to the growth of Mark's children, all of whom love her dearly. But I can not imagine that our contributions to her life could ever be compared to the ways she ministered to me.

She was the only woman who loved and missed Mark as much as I did. We spent endless hours crying on each other's shoulders. I consider her to be one of my best friends now. She and Dad McCarthy have both encouraged me in the dating field and have never made me feel as though dating or remarriage would in any way cause them to doubt the sincerity of my love for Mark. Their love for me has anchored me while giving me wings and the freedom to fly again. But some logistical issues I had to face alone.

Setting up my home without Mark made questions arise which seemed to have no answers. Do our Academy diplomas still hang together with our plaque and saber as they had for 10 years? Does the wife of a deceased F-16 pilot still splatter her decor with F-16 mementos? And what should I do with all Mark's personal things? So many of the changes and how to go about them are personal to each widow. Some will leave everything and deal with it after a year of healing. Establishing and embracing my new identity quickly so I could press on and look forward with hope were therapeutic for me

I felt passionately about making some of the decisions I needed to make quickly so my decisions would not be influenced by any future relationships. To do so, I instituted what I call "the uncompromisables." These are displays of Mark's memory which, I felt, honored Mark and the impact he had in our lives. These were minimum reminders of Mark which I believed must be maintained to acknowledge the past, a necessary ingredient to insuring a healthy adjustment for me and my children to whatever the future would hold.

I consolidated most of Mark's memorabilia, in order to make room some day for a new relationship. I had large vivid collages made up with the best photos of each child with Mark. The children have hung them proudly and prominently in their bedrooms. I had the diamonds removed from my engagement, wedding and anniversary rings, and the bands melted down to consolidate them all on a ring on my right hand. I established a "trunk of memories" for each of us which included Mark's flight suits, Air Force memorabilia, special hand-written notes, his jewelry, and articles of clothing that Mark wore in some of the special photos we had of him. I tried to put together things the children could sift through when they reached those tumultuous teen years and they attempt to establish their own identities, things they could sift through again with their own children to tell them who their grandfather was. Then I gave Mark's and my siblings and parents special items for remembrances.

All of these initial adjustments were, at times, excruciating, since the pain was so fresh and the changes were ones I did not even want to make. But, in retrospect, they dim in comparison to the mighty work God would do in my heart over the next few years.

More Than a Mother

This is a story of tragedy turned beautiful;
    of a woman's radiance in her darkest hour.
Although she's a woman I thought I'd known for years,
    I had no idea of the depth of her character.
Until through my deepest pain and hers, we were united;
    bound through grief, in heart and spirit.
You see, I lost my husband, my lover, my best friend
    a brief twelve years after we'd met.
But my mother-in-law lost her baby boy, her pride and joy,
    just thirty-one short years after his birth.
Our loss could have been the wedge which drove us apart;
    we could have gone our separate ways,
But for the love of a caring woman, "Mom" to me,
    who understood the essence of family.
During a time when she could have hidden away,
    and turned inward in her grief and sorrow,
Mom freely shared her home, her life, her memories
    and sacrificially poured out her love on me.
Even though the man who'd made us "in-laws" was gone,
    Mom adopted me and loved me as her own flesh.
We spent a year laughing, crying, and remembering together.
    Side by side, united, we faced a year of firsts.
As I awkwardly and reluctantly went on my first date,
    She was there, to watch my kids and push me out the door.
Not once have I doubted that she wants the best for me,
    for she has faithfully encouraged me to seek fulfillment,
Even though she knows in order for me to move on,
    I must move past my complete devotion to her son.
I have spent many hours thanking God for putting her in my life.
    He alone knew that she was the one I needed for healing.
Through her selfless love, she has become one of my heroines.
    She is, and always will be, more than a mother to me.

                        Mother's Day 1996

Section Two:

Press Up

Trust Me

When life seems out of control,
    Trust Me, I AM in control.
When the waiting seems too long,
    Trust Me, I AM in the silence.
When the plan has gone all wrong,
    Trust Me, I AM working out a higher plan.
When you can't see Me keeping my promises,
    Trust Me, I AM faithful.
When the burden seems too great to bear,
    Trust Me, I AM able to bear it for you.
When the pain seems too deep,
    Trust Me, I AM the Great Physician.
When you wonder if I hear your prayers,
    Trust Me, I AM always listening.

When it makes absolutely no sense,
    Trust Me, because I AM.

                January 1999

Chapter 4

Impressed by God:
Finding Legs of Faith

"For no matter how many promises God has made, they are "Yes" in Christ. And so through Him the "Amen" is spoken by us to the glory of God." II Corinthians 1:20

Weeks slowly stretched into months and those who had held me up emotionally and physically began to thin out. As annoying as the realization was, my friends and family did have lives of their own to which they had to return. Their lives resumed with some sense of normalcy. In stark contrast was my life, still consumed by my grief and completely foreign to me. At about four months after Mark's death, I was settled in my new home and there were no major changes ahead which I could hope would ease the pain, just the day in and day out chore of facing life as a parent of three without Mark. And to make matters worse, little by little, the realization of the size of the task before me had begun to sink in. It looked enormously bleak and lonely.

The adrenaline surges that had hindered productive sleep during the first few months began to dwindle. Once they left, I recognized that they had been a blessing in disguise because they had kept me going, giving me the energy to do all I had needed to do. But without them, sleep was now an escape. Just getting myself out of bed was a struggle. It was at this turning point that questions of God's ability to sustain me over the long haul began to creep in. I knew God had been with me for the fourteen years before Mark died, and I had sensed His loving arms wrapped tightly around me during those first few months after Mark's death, but could He be enough for me in the long years ahead?

Finding Faith

We often glibly pronounce that "God is sufficient," but I wondered if He could *really* be all that I needed. And if He could be enough, what part would I need to play to allow Him the room to be? I frequently pondered the reality of God's ability to keep His promises. I knew that He had not let me down so far, but I had not felt as if I needed Him as much either. So it was desperation that drove me to the understanding that perhaps what I needed to do was to somehow let go and trust Him now. This would mean giving up some of my self-sufficiency and somehow forging a new trail, unfamiliar to my proud, independent self. I would need to learn to lean on Him in practical, physical ways.

Faith is a funny thing. If God were someone concrete and physical that we could see in His full glory and power, then to trust Him would be easy, but it would not require faith. But God wants us to trust Him, to step out in faith, believing some pretty incredible things about Him without ever seeing Him, without even having a two way conversation with Him. God, through the book of Hebrews defines faith this way:

"Now faith is being sure of what we hope for and certain of what we do not see." Hebrews 11:1

Faith goes against all our physical senses. Faith requires stepping out of our comfort zone. But over and over again in the Bible we see God rewarding those with great faith. *A faithful heart is the venue God uses to display His miraculous powers.* Faith is what allows us to enjoy the security and power of a relationship with Him. Abraham believed God's promise that he would be the father of many nations, even though his *"body was as good as dead - since he was about one hundred years old - and that Sarah's womb was also dead."(Romans 4:18, 19).* He was blessed beyond belief because of his faith:

"Yet he [Abraham] *did not waiver through unbelief regarding the promise of God, but was strengthened in his faith and gave glory to God, being fully persuaded that God had power to do what He had promised." Romans 4:20-21*

Another example of great faith was the centurion who came to Jesus to have his paralyzed servant healed. Jesus responded that He would go and heal him. But the centurion somehow recognized Jesus as God in all his power and holiness. He showed Jesus his faith first by recognizing his unworthiness to even have the living Christ come into his home. Then he told Jesus that He did not need to go with him because he recognized that Jesus' authority was not limited by His location. He was fully convinced that all Jesus needed to do was say the word and his servant would be healed. The centurion's actions showed what he really believed. What was Jesus' response to this man of great faith?

"When Jesus heard this, He was astonished and said to those following Him, ' I tell you the truth, I have not found anyone in Israel with such great faith.'" (Matthew 8:10)

Can you imagine having Jesus astounded at your faith? Both the story of Abraham and the story of the centurion motivate me to want to become a woman of faith. So I determined in my heart that I would not limit God's power in my life by my own definitions of Him. Instead, I wanted to allow God to reign with all His strength and might over every area of my future life. I also knew that faith crumbles with spotters or crutches. There is an old analogy that you can *believe* a chair will hold you, but *faith* is sitting down in that chair. I would submit that most of us put a cushion under the chair so we will not get hurt if it breaks. The fact that we put the cushion there is proof that we do not really trust the chair to hold us. We often say we have faith in God but then pad our lives so that, if God fails, we have a backup. We are comfortable mixing God-reliance with self-reliance. *But the truth and power of God and His Word will not be evident in our lives until we stand on them and burn all our other bridges.*

God versus Psychology

As I began to step out in my faith, one of my greatest frustrations came from well meaning, compassionate Christians, who would say, "Well, you have your faith, but..." and then go on to cite some "psychological fact" over which God had no power. I knew they were just trying to empathize with how hard my situation must be, but if God is really who He says He is, then there is nothing over which He does not have jurisdiction. So I chose, instead, to bank my life on scripture being true and I was not going to let even well meaning Christians talk me out of it. One of the scriptures

62

I decided I would lean on heavily was I Thessalonians 4:13-14:

"Brothers, we do not want you to be ignorant about those who fall asleep, or grieve like the rest of men, who have no hope. We believe Jesus died and rose again and so we believe that God will bring with Jesus those who have fallen asleep in Him."

I Thess 4:13-14

During the pursuit of my master's degree in counseling, I had been exposed to the psychology of grief and the steps most people go through in grieving. I decided not to pull those out and read them. They were steps determined by men in trying to understand the mind of man. They were written from the observations of men and women who had seen and counseled thousands of grieving clients.

While they might be helpful for the counselor trying to determine the emotional state of his client, or for those helping a grieving friend through her trials, they were not for me. Men, albeit well intentioned men, wrote them. I decided I would not let men, who study men's minds from the outside, shape my future when I had the creator, and sustainer of *my* mind to whom I could listen. If God did not want me to *grieve as those who had no hope*, then He must have a plan for the ways that I needed to grieve. I decided I would count on Him to take me through whatever steps I needed to go through for healing, no more and no less.

Hope Reconstructed

Definitely when I lost Mark, many of my hopes and dreams for this lifetime were lost with him. But the anchor and the source of my hopes for this life, as well as the next, was God and He could not be taken from me. He promised to always remain with me:

"No one whose hope is in You;
will ever be put to shame." Psalms 25:3

"...God has said, 'Never will I leave you;
Never will I forsake you.'" Hebrews 13:5

My hope needed to be reconstructed, and I knew from my civil engineering background that any remodeling job is a messy, painful process. When one is remodeling even one small room, the entire house is affected. Even rooms that are closed off and are seemingly immune from the mess get dusty. There was that kind of ripple effect in my life when Mark died. Areas I thought would remain "normal" became messy as well. A new "normal" had to be established. What God needed to accomplish was an emotional paradigm shift. And what I needed to do was to let Him have free reign in making that shift. Hanging on to my former hope would not help that. My hope and my joy must come from God and the future He had prepared for me even before my birth.

"For we are God's workmanship, created in Christ Jesus to do
good works, which God prepared in advance for us to do."
Ephesians 2:10

But as I armed myself with this truth from God, many of my friends, both Christians and non-Christians thought I was in denial. The truth is that I understood what I had lost more than they could ever know, but I was intent on hanging onto God's promises:

"'For I know the plans I have for you,' declares the Lord,
'plans to prosper you and not to harm you, plans to give you

hope and a future. Then you will call upon me, and come and pray to me, and I will listen to you. You will seek me and find me when you seek me with all your heart. I will be found by you.'" Jeremiah 29:11-12 (NIV)

Looking for God's Plan

God has a plan for my life. Mark's death is somehow part of that plan. His plan is to prosper me and give me a future. I clung to this promise like plastic wrap clings to glass. I am excited to see what things He might want to do with my life and how He might be able to use me. The verse also made it clear that I had a part in the plan: to seek God with all my heart. God promised I would find Him, and what a promise that is! So I went on a "quest." I bought a new Bible, and I set out to get to know God with all my heart, a quest I am still on today. And God is gracious, for rather than overwhelming me; He shows me more of Himself, little by little. This book is a product of God's faithfully revealing Himself to me since Mark's death, as I have sought Him. I have found Him to be trustworthy. He is the original "promise keeper":

"The Lord is a refuge for the oppressed,
a stronghold in times of trouble.
Those who know your name will trust you,
For you, Lord, have never forsaken those who seek you."
Psalm 9: 9-10 (NIV)

I can read and understand this verse, even say I believe it, but what I truly believe is fleshed out in my life. I can not honestly tell God I believe Mark is in heaven, and I believe He has a higher plan for my life, then wallow in my own little pity party. There were times when I felt myself sinking into a depressive state. During those times, I had to go to God so often that I could not count the trips. I had read through these and other scriptures to remind myself just who God is, how much He loves me, and how He has a higher plan for my life. This was my practical, physical way of standing on God's promises. They are here to offer us His power, but we often do not go to the scriptures to recall truth when it is the best thing for us, because we *want* to have a pity party. I will be the first to admit that in my rebellious spirit, there were times I chose to have a pity party. I just felt like being self-absorbed and angry with God for His apparent unfairness. The result? Loneliness, bitterness, and out of control emotions consumed me.

No More Pity Parties

After many pity parties, I finally figured out pity parties never helped me one bit. Not everyone agrees with this opinion. I had a widow tell me once that when her Christian husband died, she determined to "experience the awfulness of his death." What followed was a deep depression. She said it was as if she fell into a deep hole and was not sure she would ever get out. That is *grieving like one who has no hope!* We can go there if we want to, but God does not want us to. He will eventually drag us out of the mire if we choose to take that route, but He has given us hope in Him so we do not have to ever let our feet touch the mire.

Standing on God's promises does not come natural to us; it is supernatural. One of the first promises I decided to stand on had to do with my children. Friends and family have been faithful to point out to me God's provision for the widow and the fatherless:

"A father to the fatherless, a defender of widows, is God in his holy dwelling." Psalm 68:5 (NIV)

God promised to be the father of my children. Study after study shows that children reared in a single parent family are much more likely to be involved in crime, to suffer from some form of addiction, and to live a promiscuous life style. Statistics about girls reared without a father can be especially frightening. But God has promised to be *a father to the fatherless*. That means I have two choices: I can worry about the emotional state of my children, looking for signs that they are headed for their inevitably terrible fate, or I can trust that God will really be all my children need in a father to grow up emotionally healthy.

A Pragmatic God

The truths He gives us are not merely solid theology; they are practical and useful for everyday life. When my young daughter cries for a father, my response shows what I truly believe. If I can stand in faith, I can tell her, honestly, that I would like to some day have another husband to be her father, but we will always have the best Daddy ever, our Heavenly Father, who loves us more than any human is able. Then she will not grow up thinking of herself as fatherless.

I saw God fulfilling His promise to me and to Bryan about a year after his father's death. Bryan had taken a shower and he had obviously had some thinking time during the peace and quiet of this solitary task. As he opened the shower door, he blurted out, "Hey Mom, you know we have the best Dad in the whole world?" Unsure of what he was referring to I said, "We do?" He replied confidently, "Yup, our Dad is faster, bigger and stronger than Batman and Superman put together, 'cause our Dad is God!" I yearn to live my life trusting God as my young children do. This is a truth every child ought to grow up with, regardless of whether he has an earthly father or not. Most of us will lose our earthly father at some time during our lives. How reassuring to know that we will never be Fatherless.

God as my Husband

It is obvious in scripture that God has a special place in His heart for the vulnerable. He not only comforts the fatherless with His presence, He is the defender of the widow, and "He's bigger and stronger than Batman and Superman put together." But He also reminds us that in addition to being our defender, He is our husband:

> "For your Maker is your husband –
> The Lord Almighty is His name –
> The Holy One of Israel is your Redeemer;
> He is called the God of all the earth." Isaiah 54:5

You have probably heard that one before. The pastor's wife, in an attempt to comfort, reminds you that God will be your husband. As much as you like her, it is hard not to mumble under your breath, "Yea, that's easy for you to say, you have a real husband." I know because I mumbled something similar myself. But what if it is true, I wondered. What if He can really fulfill me as a husband? I knew I did not want to let my pride get in His way. Once again, God got a hold of my heart and showed me that He really wanted to be my husband. I did not have the faith of Abraham when He first pointed this out, because I

68

wanted a man to hug me, to keep me warm at night and to do the manly chores around my house.

It was much easier for me to tell the children that God was their Father than to buy into the fact that God could be my husband. He may not have been all I wanted, but He was definitely all I needed, once I let Him be. I decided that if God were serious about being my husband, then I ought to be, too. I looked for ways to get to know Him intimately. I remembered the love letters, the epistles that had been written to me in the New Testament. I went through them, writing down all the qualities of my new husband that were written in those letters. It was not long into that exercise that I began to grasp how unworthy I was to be His bride. I have a husband who listens to everything I ever said. I have a husband who is always there, who never misses a birthday or a special event. But most importantly, I have a husband who loves me perfectly, regardless of how I respond. I will be the first to admit this is a hard truth to flesh out, but it is worth the effort. Those lonely hours after I had put the children to bed, I would sit and be with God, my lover and my husband. I would read His letters to me and I would share with Him the struggles of the day.

Those of us who are grieving face a real temptation to fill our voids with anything so that we do not feel the pain and the emptiness. We are vulnerable. But eating, drinking, carousing, sleeping, and taking exotic vacations will not fill the emptiness. In the end they only exacerbate the feelings of isolation and make us feel worse about ourselves. We have to choose to fill the void with a relationship with someone who is perfectly trustworthy with our vulnerabilities. God is real. He really can do everything He promises. We have to be brave enough to allow Him to fill the voids that seem so enormous in our lives. It is an effort and it takes faith:

> *"For no matter how many promises God has made, they are "Yes" in Christ. And so through him the "Amen" is spoken by us to the glory of God. Now it is God who makes both us and you stand firm in Christ. He anointed us, set His seal of ownership on us, and put his Spirit in our hearts as a deposit, guaranteeing what is to come."*   II Cor 1:20-22

To God, With Love

How can I possibly write a love letter
to the One who's name is "Love"?
For I know the love I have for You
is but a poor reflection of Your love for me.
All my words of love, straight from the heart,
regardless of their eloquence and depth,
dim in the shadow of Your pure, brilliant love:
a love which knows no bounds.
Yet I will struggle to write of my love
and learn through my own inadequacy.
For only when I squarely face my own weakness
can I begin to comprehend the fullness of Your love.

You have been my stronghold
the One in whom I put my trust.
When all other relationships fade away,
You remain with me, always.
You have loved me when I'm unlovable:
You have been faithful through my unfaithfulness.
You alone have seen the depth of my ugliness:
and found beauty in me when no one else could.
You have listened to my continuous grumbling:
and the accusations I've thrown at you in ignorance.
You have never forced Your love on me,
but have waited patiently for me to accept it.

There is no doubt that Your love for me
is completely undeserved.
Rather, it is a gift you have given me, freely
for I have no means to earn it.
Your unconditional love for me
is what I desire above life, itself.
Without it, I am but an empty vessel
which can never be adequately filled.
But my love for You has limitless potential
as long as it reflects You, Love itself.
I love You, God, with all my heart.
May I strive to be worthy of Your love for me.

Valentine's Day 1996

But Still...

We Christians have a saying; I've said it oft myself,
With one side of our mouths we lift praises to God,
We say we adore His attributes;
We exalt His precepts;
We acknowledge His authority;
We laud His power.
But out of the other side of our mouths, we mutter,
      "but still..."
And we limit God's truths in our lives with our very words.

"God I know You said You are love,
      but still there is no love left..."
"God I know You said not to worry,
      but still what if..."
"God I know You told me to walk this way,
      but still my path feels right..."
"God I know You are all powerful,
      but still I can't..."

The limits we place on God are our own.
The truth is God has no *"but stills..."*
God's attributes are perfect and perfectly available.
God's precepts are flawless and worthy of our obedience.
God's authority is sovereign and deserves our submission.
God's power is limitless and accessible to His children.
The fullness of God is evident not in our *"but stills..."*
But rather in our *"ands..."*

"God I know You said you are love,
    and I will love as You do.."
"God I know You said not to worry,
    and I lay my concerns at Your feet..."
"God I know You told me to walk this way,
    and I will do it even when it's hard..."
"God I know You are all powerful,
    and I seek Your power to do Your will..."

Singing praises to God is commendable;
But how we live proves what we really believe.
Let us illustrate God's attributes;
Let us live His precepts;
Let us answer to His authority;
Let us walk in His power.
If we can believe God's truths "*and*..."
Then there will be no more "*but stills*" left for us to hang on
    to.

Summer 1996,
Revised February 2001

Chapter 5

The Power Press:
God's Omnipotence

"We were under great pressure, far beyond our ability to endure, so that we despaired even of life. Indeed, in our hearts we felt the sentence of death. But this happened that we might not rely on ourselves but on God, who raises the dead."

II Corinthians 1:8-9

I had said it many times before, I am sure, but for some reason, this time I heard myself say it, "But still..." It fits so reasonably into even the most mature Christian's speech. In an attempt to be sympathetic, realistic and compassionate, we say it all the time. We have a great fear of "over-spiritualizing" everything, especially when we are ministering to people in hard circumstances. I wrote the poem "But Still..." because I realized my use of those words was limiting God's power to be all He can be and do all He wants to do in my life. Once I heard myself saying it, I recognized the phrase in many of my conversations:

I know a fruit of the Spirit is patience, God, *but still* the kids are acting demon-possessed, and I am just a naturally impatient person, *You* made me that way.

I know You said You would be husband to the husbandless, *but still* I need a *real* husband.

God, I understand You think I should forgive, *but still* I just can not seem to bring myself to forgive her for betraying me.

The Power of Faith

Once again, I am able to take any truth from the Bible and see how much I really believe that truth to be true by the way I am living. I am convinced that we, as Christians, have much more power available to us than we use. We are wimpy Christians. *He is not a wimpy God we serve. God is as powerful in our lives as we allow Him to be.* Certainly, He has the power to do anything He pleases in our lives even against our will, but God delights in exhibiting His power through a heart yielded to Him, through a heart that truly believes He keeps His promises:

> *"And he [Jesus] did not do many miracles there because of their lack of faith."*　　　　　Matthew 13:58

God's truths are powerful, yes, even miraculous. We see their power when we learn God's promises to us, learn His precepts, learn His attributes and then learn to stand on them. We will not stand on them when we spout them off only to follow them up with a "but still..." as I was doing. We have to have the courage to follow them up with an "and..." instead.

Powerful Fruit

Take the fruit of the Spirit for example:

> *"So I say, live by the Spirit, and you will not gratify the desires of the sinful nature...The fruit of the Spirit is love, joy, peace, patience, kindness, goodness, faithfulness, gentleness and self-control." Galatians 5:16 & 22*

I guess I have always seen the fruit of the Spirit like the fruits at the grocery store. Take what you like and leave

76

the rest for someone else.   I enjoy kiwi, bananas, strawberries, cantaloupe and grapes (to name a few). I do not care much for grapefruit, papaya, and lemons. I buy only the fruits I want to eat. So I thought it was with the fruits of the Spirit.   I occasionally exhibit love, peace, kindness, goodness, faithfulness, and self-control, but I have real problems with joy, patience and gentleness.   I figured I would display those fruits I am good at and someone else in the body of Christ could display the rest. But God has shown me that I was "but stilling..." the fruits of the Spirit and losing God's power in my life by choosing not to believe what God said is true.

God showed me, "Patti, I said, 'The fruit of the Spirit *IS* love, joy, peace, patience, kindness, goodness, faithfulness, gentleness, and self-control."   I did not say, 'Sometimes the fruit of the Spirit is...' or 'The fruit of the Spirit in some people is...' I said, 'The fruit of the Spirit *IS*...'" So these are the fruits of His Spirit, all of them. When I am choosing to be sullen, impatient or harsh, then I am gratifying the desires of my sinful nature; I am walking in my flesh, period. I say "Lord You say the fruit of the Spirit is joy, *but still* how can You expect me to be joyful when my husband just died?" If I proceed to be sullen and bitter, then I am choosing to walk in my sinful nature rather than in the Spirit. The fruit of the Spirit *IS* joy.

I can enjoy walking in God's joy if I follow that assertion with "*and* I will walk in Your joy by sitting at Your feet, choosing to think of all I have to be thankful for and basking in the hope of Your promises." *There is power in believing God even when He does not seem to make sense. It is faith in its purest form and God loves faith and honors the faithful with His power.* We do not have the ability to be joyful in our flesh at the death of a loved one, but the Spirit does. He dwells within us waiting for us to call on Him. Choosing to say, "Lord, I believe you *and* here's how I'm going to live it..." opens up a world of divine power. As II Corinthians 1:9 tells us, *"this happened that we might not rely on ourselves but on God, who raises the dead."*

The Unlimited Power of God

We must understand that the power comes from God but His desire is that we would live powerful lives. Here is what Paul prayed for the Ephesians:

"I pray also that the eyes of your heart may be enlightened in order that you may know the hope to which he has called you, the riches of his glorious inheritance in the saints, and his incomparably great power for us who believe. That power is like the working of his mighty strength, which he exerted in Christ when he raised him from the heavenly realms. Far above all rule and authority, power and dominion, and every title that can be given, not only in the present age but also in the one to come."   Ephesians 1:18-21

That is the kind of power we have available to us to live godly, upright, joyful and hopeful lives, power like that of the resurrection. There is no power on this earth that can make the dead come back to life. With all our technology, we can not prevent death or reverse it. But God has all power. That kind of power is available to us to live the kind of lives God has called us to live. Both Peter and Paul were sure that God's power was sufficient for us:

"His divine power has given us everything we need for life and godliness through our knowledge of Him who called us by His own glory and goodness."   2 Peter 1:3

"And God is able to make all grace abound to you so that in all things, and at all times, having all that you need, you will abound in every good work."   2 Corinthians 9:8

God's power is available in every area of our lives, even when it does not *seem* as if it is. He said His power gives us *everything* we need for life and godliness. Do I have the faith to really believe that? Is God big enough to help me through my financial struggles or can He only accomplish small things like the creation of this universe? Can God provide *everything* my children and I need to work through our grief and adjust to living without our father and mate? We said before that faith is like sitting on a chair. You can say you believe it will hold you, but faith is plopping down in the chair. And, although we exercise it daily, faith in a chair is really unfounded. Chairs have been known to break or topple. God has kept every promise He has ever made! He cannot lie. **God is the only One is this life who is completely trustworthy.** Plop down in the "chair of God" with full confidence.

Living the Power of God

This sounds good in theory, but how, realistically, do we learn to trust God thoroughly enough to plop down in His chair? We have to spend time with Him to allow Him a chance to earn our trust. That means blocking out time to spend with Him in reading His Word, listening to Him and praying. We want to ignore this step, but it cannot be skipped. We would rather step out in faith without getting our marching orders. But the relationship is vital:

"I am the vine; you are the branches. If a man remains in me and I in him, he will bear much fruit; apart from me, you can do nothing."   *John 15:5*

We have divine power *with* God; we can do nothing *without* Him. Can any other relationship be as vital as the one we have with God? Through faith I believe my relationship with God is worth building. We build a relationship with God the same way we build one with anyone else, by giving Him our time. We read the love letters He sent us over and over again. We wake up early to meet with Him or stay up late looking for a chance to be with Him. We guard our time alone with Him jealously.

Obedience Builds Trust

But we can not just sit in our rooms and be in perfect fellowship with Him forever because He is active in this world, and He has invited us to join Him and work alongside of Him. It is when we step out in obedience that we allow God's truths to have a chance to become alive to us and to be proven true. We have to walk what He says is true. This is one of the great paradoxes of the Christian life. It is hard to step out if you do not trust God, and you can not learn to trust God until you are willing to step out:

"Jesus said, 'If you hold to my teaching, you are really my disciples. Then you will know the truth and the truth will set you free.'"   *John 8:31-32*

"Whoever has my commands and obeys them, he is the one who loves me, he who loves me will be loved by my Father, and I too will love him and show myself to him." *John 14:21*

Notice the pattern of the above verses: obedience first, then revelation. We have to be willing to walk in obedience to the teachings of the scriptures before the scales of our eyes can fall off and we can know how true they are! Then the truth of those scriptures will free us and God will reveal Himself to us more clearly. It is a big circle: we spend time with God; then we step out on His truths; then we see they are true and God is trustworthy; God reveals more of Himself to us; we want to know Him better so we spend more time with God. I have found the character of the God who wrote the Word to be completely trustworthy, and every pass I am privileged to make around the circle builds the trust.

Waves of Doubt

Unfortunately, my life has not been one long trip on the circle of faith in God. Even though God is trustworthy and completely faithful, I have not been so faithful to Him. I have experienced waves of doubt. But God knows our hearts. He knows our thoughts before we think them and is fully aware of the doubts we have about Him. I believe even the most faithful saints have doubts at some time.

At times for me, doubting seems absurd, especially when I consider the vastness of the universe, the masses of humanity, the complexity of the human body, the variety of the known species, or the origins of life. When I take time to ponder these things, the evidence for an intelligent creator who is infinitely more brilliant and capable than I am is overwhelmingly substantiated. I often have to go back to remind myself of these undeniable proofs when I begin to doubt. Still, amazingly, doubt sweeps over me anyway more often that I would care to admit, especially in this book! I have found that admitting these doubts to God helps me know my relationship with Him is real.

We have no other model in our lives for such a relationship as we have with God. We do not tell anyone all our thoughts or emotions; doing so would not be wise, considerate or helpful. But suppose someone knew all our thoughts and we still refused to admit to having them. My children do this sometimes, when I have seen something they have done and they refuse to admit it. It harms the relationship because then I know my child has lied to me. This is how I think of my doubts about God; just admitting them to Him alone shows I have faith that He heard them. Sometimes, just my admission will point out the error in my logic and quench my doubts. But most of the time, it leads me to question God in the area I have doubts. I believe God loves to answer respectful, genuine hearts that are seeking His truths:

"If any of you lacks wisdom, he should ask God, who gives generously to all without finding fault." James 1:5

"No Fault" Questions

Our teachers and our parents used to say there was "no such thing as a dumb question." But then you would ask a question and the look on their faces showed you had managed to ask the first dumb question ever. Well, God made the "no such thing as a dumb question" promise to us in the above verse, but thankfully, He meant it. I think that is because God desires our faith over our intelligence and the fact that we simply come to Him with the question and believe He can provide an answer is faith. I am thankful God allows "no fault" questions. I believe His promise *and* continually ask God questions to seek His wisdom.

Some of the questions I have asked are some of the same ones you have probably asked:

How can God be loving and allow hatred to prevail on this world?

How can God be just when He allows babies to be born into poverty?

How do we know God's Word is true?

Any Christian with open eyes has asked questions similar to these. God is big enough to answer every question, but, often, when God reveals Himself to me, my revelation includes understanding that my question was missing the mark. Is that not what we see in so many of Jesus' answers during His life? His reply does not necessarily answer the question, but because He knows our hearts, He responds to what He sees there. That is why we have to listen carefully.

God's answers are as incredible as He is. As I have searched God and His scripture for answers to some questions similar to those above, His "I AM" response kept getting in the way of the answers I was sure God would give me. "I AM." This is the name God used to describe Himself through Moses to the Israelites so they would know it was their God. It was also the phrase Jesus used when answering His accusers:

"Again the high priest asked him, 'Are you the Christ, the Son of the Blessed One?'

'I am,' said Jesus. 'And you will see the Son of Man sitting at the right hand of the Mighty One and coming on the clouds of heaven.'

The high priest tore his clothes. 'Why do we need any more witnesses?' he asked. You have heard the blasphemy.'"

Mark 14:61-64

"I AM." Is it not just like God to come up with a simple name that says more than we could even imagine? That is the answer I kept getting as I asked so many questions to God. And it took quite a while, but it finally began meaning something to me. I have heard it said you can fill in the blank, "I AM _____," with your need, because God can provide all your needs. But He was teaching me something new about Himself. I knew the scripture in which God is described as love:

"God is love." I John 4:16.

If that is the case, we are silly to question whether God is acting loving in a situation, because He defines what love is. Therefore, by definition, everything God does is loving. We need to learn what love is by observing God. I began to wonder about all the other attributes we question God about, His justice, mercy, goodness, righteousness, wisdom and truth. Perhaps, He defines those as well. As I searched the scriptures, I found this to be true. Not only is every good gift from His hand, God Himself defines all that is good. Therefore, in studying what is true, my best source is to be with Truth, Himself. This revelation freed me to stop critiquing God and instead, to tuck myself under His wing as an apprentice with the Master and learn all I could learn. Faith is required to believe this and more is necessary to walk in it.

I still question God; the questioning did not stop with this revelation, but how I question is what has changed:

God, I know you are love. Teach me about Your love which allows hatred to prevail on this world.

God I know you are Justice.   Train me to understand how justice is shown even in the midst of babies being born into poverty.

God I know You are truth.   Let me learn all that is true from Your Word.

Yes, God is able to teach those with teachable hearts. We must understand that God has more to teach than we can ever grasp. *At one time I sought God as a <u>means</u> to any worthwhile <u>end</u>. Since then, I have discovered God <u>is</u> the worthwhile <u>end</u> and His presence enables His <u>means</u> to become mine.*

The Great I AM

The other day I interrogated God,
"You say You are WISE, TRUE, JUST and LOVING."
"How can it be WISE to let evil thrive in this world?"
"Can everything in your Word be TRUE?"

He seemed to listen silently, so I continued,
"What is JUST about allowing innocent illness and death?"
"How can You LOVE the unsaved and send them to Hell?"
As I waited for His profound insight, He only answered, "I AM."

And God taught me through His Word,
If He really is the great I AM,
Then His attributes do not define Him,
Rather He is the definition of those attributes.

God does not just make wise decisions.
God is WISDOM.
I am able to sit at the feet of a perfect mind,
And He molds my mind to think wisely.

God does not only speak truth.
God is TRUTH.
I can gaze on everything true as I fix my eyes on Him.
And what is counterfeit will reveal itself.

God is not merely a just ruler.
God is JUSTICE.
I have been given the honor of sitting in His court,
And absorbing what true justice is.

God is not just a perfect lover,
God is LOVE.
I am able to bask in all aspects of His matchless love,
And allow Him to fashion my heart to beat as His.

If I believe this, I no longer need to ask,
"God, are You WISE, TRUE, JUST and LOVING in this situation?"
But "Lord help me through this situation to better grasp
What true WISDOM, TRUTH, JUSTICE and LOVE are."

God is not limited as I am.
God, Himself, defines the very attributes I seek to understand.
I am best able to exhibit His perfect attributes,
As I simply pursue the Great I AM.

February 2000

Whatever It Takes

I came before You Lord
    exhausted and alone,
    at the end of my rope.
Believing that if You didn't answer my prayer
    in my timing;
    in my way,
I would surely fall from the end of the rope
    into the abyss of darkness,
    far from Your presence.

So I waited for Your saving hand to rescue me,
    to gently hold me,
    to pull me back up.
But You didn't come as I had asked,
    so I clung to the rope,
    until I reached the end of my strength.
Then, in desperation, I shook my fist at You,
    losing my grip, I fell,
    lower than I've ever been before.

From the depths of darkness,
    I saw You clearly,
    I heard Your voice.
In ways I couldn't have from above,
    I felt Your loving touch,
    You became real to me.
I saw the love in Your eyes
    As You constantly watched me,
    and I finally understood.

You had a plan all along
     to draw me to Yourself;
     to show me Your love.
I couldn't have seen it
     or felt it
     or experienced it,
If You had answered my prayer,
     in my timing;
     in my way.

Now, when I'm at the end of my rope,
     I have a new prayer;
     I have a new excitement.
For I can look expectantly at how
     You will show Yourself to me
     in fresh, creative ways.
My new prayer is one of trust
     because You have proven Yourself
     to be trustworthy.

I can pray confidently to You, my loving Father,
     "Lord, draw me near to Yourself,

     Whatever it takes."

September 1997

90

Chapter 6

Compressed from Above:
Ways of the Father

"For my thoughts are not your thoughts, neither are your ways my ways," declares the Lord. "As the heavens are higher than the earth, so are my ways higher than your ways and my thoughts than your thoughts."

Isaiah 55:8-9

Marty Staton was nine years old. Being a typical seventeen-year-old, I did not give him the time of day. His oldest sister, Terry, had been my best friend since the seventh grade. She and I were inseparable. That day we were at the pool. Looking back, it is amazing I ever made it to the pool; in those days I was so enamored with studying myself in the mirror. My parents teased me by saying that the first three words I ever spoke in this world were "Me, me, me." It is funny to say now but I had not managed to find much else more important in my first decade and a half of living than myself.

Somehow that day I was able to tear myself away from the mirror long enough to make it to the pool. I was standing at the bottom of the high dive. Marty was cowering up on the board, unable to make himself jump. I yelled some encouraging words like, "Chicken!" and "It's just water, Marty, it won't hurt you!" He wanted to jump so badly, but that first step was terrifying and he could not bring himself to do it. "Jump or get down, Marty. There are people waiting you know," I sympathized. I had my sweet jack knife to perform and he was getting in my way. Humiliated and defeated, Marty reluctantly climbed back down the ladder and slunk over to his waiting towel. I was too self-absorbed to notice how his defeat must have affected him.

The next day Terry called me to tell me Marty had been riding his bike and had been struck by a car, killing him instantly. Just like that, he was dead. My last conversation with him seared through my breaking heart. The finality of that conversation was an incredible tutor. Never would I have the chance to hug his scrawny shoulders and tell him he was okay for a nine-year-old. Nor would I have the opportunity to tell him that Terry was lucky to have him for a brother or how much I enjoyed his mischievous little grin and dancing eyes. All of the positive thoughts I had about Marty but never shared with him for whatever reason now accumulated in my throat like a terrible case of indigestion, mounting whenever I was brave enough to face them.

God at Work

The greatest miracle of my life was accelerated because of Marty's life and his death. His family knew the Lord and was faithful to Him through Marty's death. I saw a peace in their family in the midst of what seemed to be a senseless death. They were sure God knew what He was doing even though it did not make sense to them. ***They mourned and they wept, but they believed God.*** Theirs was a faith like none that I had ever seen. It was a faith that made a powerful difference in their lives. It was a trusting relationship unlike my religion. It caught my attention. About a year and a half later, God brought me from death to life as I acknowledged my own need for a personal Savior and professed Jesus as my Lord. I do not believe God allowed Marty to die just for me, but He definitely used Marty's death in my life to draw me to Himself. In typical God-style, He took a tragedy and made something beautiful.

Who knew, other than God, that Marty's death would have such a profound impact on my life? Who would have guessed that fifteen years later I would be faced with walking through my own similar deep loss? All I know is that, when I lost Mark, I *knew* God would sustain me, and that He knew what He was doing, even if it did not make sense to me. I saw that it was true for the Statons, and I believed that it would be true for me.

No Mistake

Three days after Mark's crash, we went to our little Baptist church. Pastor Oscar Barrow, who had been with me constantly the last few days, asked me if I wanted to say anything. As Marty's family had done for me, I wanted others to know that God could still be trusted. Trembling, I stood up and said thanks to all the church members who had prayed for us and rallied behind us over the last few days. Then I told them that I trusted God and I believed that, if I could go up and see the big picture that God sees, unlimited by time or space, that I too would pick this path for my family and for me.

Those were not merely words. I was sure God had a greater plan for us when He took Mark. His death was not some cosmic "Oops!" It was God moving us forward in the plan he had lovingly laid out for our lives. If I really believed this, then I would need to find ways to become excited about His plan for my life. This required me to keep a sharp focus on His eternal perspective while not becoming bogged down in what was happening to me:

"Therefore we do not lose heart. Though outwardly we are wasting away, yet inwardly we are being renewed day by day. For our light and momentary troubles are achieving for us an eternal glory that far outweighs them all. So we fix our eyes not on what is seen, but on what is unseen. For what is seen is temporary, but what is unseen is eternal."

II Corinthians 4:16-18

Outwardly I may be going through the greatest struggle of my life, but inwardly God is promising to renew me day by day as I choose to fix my gaze on something much greater than myself, God's omniscient plan. It is unseen, so it requires faith, but the rewards are eternal. And we have the perfect example:

"Let us fix our eyes on Jesus, the author and perfecter of our faith, who for the joy set before him endured the cross, scorning its shame, and sat down at the right hand of the throne of God. Consider him who endured such opposition from sinful men, so that you will not grow weary and lose heart."

Hebrews 12: 2-3

God had an eternal plan when He allowed Jesus to go to the cross. His plan allowed us to come into His presence. It is a fantastic plan, much more generous and ingenious than anything I could have ever dreamed of orchestrating. Although Jesus knew why He was enduring the cross, it was certainly no fun for Jesus. He had to keep His sights on "the joy set before him" when He would be able to usher sinners like you and me into His kingdom by cleansing us with those drops of blood He chose agonizingly to shed for us. ***If Jesus had to keep His sights on the eternal to endure earthly hardships, how much more so do we?*** So we fix our eyes on Jesus. If we feel as if we

94

have too little faith to endure, we fix our eyes on Him because He is not only the author, but He is the perfecter of our faith. Our faith originates with Jesus and He is the only one who can increase our faith.

Letting God be God

So why are we unable to see life the way God does? It seems as if it would surely make life easier if we did. But I have learned to be thankful that I do not get to run this world. It would sure be a mess if I did, since I can not see much past myself and know so little. Who is more qualified to run this world than the Creator Himself, who loves each one of us and who is *"not wanting anyone to perish but everyone to come to repentance." (II Peter 3:9)* And God is not just optimizing situations, as we would try to do to bring people to Himself. He is directing and orchestrating situations to draw each of us to Himself. He is giving us every opportunity to see Him. He knows our hearts and minds and He also knows how we will respond to Him. So He is able to factor in things we could never know or comprehend.

"'For my thoughts are not your thoughts, neither are your ways my ways,' declares the Lord. 'As the heavens are higher than the earth, so are my ways higher than your ways and my thoughts than your thoughts.'"

Isaiah 55:8-9

I want God's plan, not mine. **God's plans are trustworthy; mine are not. When things do not go my way, I'm thankful I know Whose way they are going.**

95

Habakkuk learned that God sometimes uses some unorthodox methods to reach His people. Habakkuk was complaining to God about the sinful state of His people, Israel, and asking God to do something about it. When God finally answered Habakkuk, He said he was going to raise up the Babylonians, a "ruthless and impetuous people" to sweep across the whole earth. Habakkuk had waited a long time for an answer, but he could not believe God could use such a wicked nation to punish a nation much more righteous than they. So Habakkuk was facing the annihilation of his people at the hands of a vile nation. How did Habakkuk respond?

> *"Though the fig tree does not bud and there are no grapes on the vines. Though the olive crop fails and the fields produce no food. Though there are no sheep in the pen and no cattle in the stalls, yet I will rejoice in the Lord, I will be joyful in God my Savior. The Sovereign Lord is my strength; he makes my feet like the feet of a deer, he enables me to go on the heights."*
>
> *Habakkuk 3:17-19*

Was Habakkuk in denial? How could he "rejoice in the Lord" in the face of disaster? Habakkuk had learned the secret of joyful, powerful, godly living: our state of mind will always be unstable if it is dependent upon our circumstances, but we can rise above any circumstance when our state of mind is dependent solely on the character of God. If we put our hope in anyone else or in any circumstance to bring us joy, we will be continuously disappointed. We can put our hope in any of the promises God has made, but the only thing He promises constantly and immediately is Himself. And He is enough to give us joy and hope through any trial or circumstance. *We have a* tendency to focus our eyes on our circumstances despite God's omnipotent, sovereign presence in our lives. But what we need to learn to do is focus our eyes on our omnipotent, sovereign God despite our circumstances. God is sufficient. He always comes through.

Job's Example

I was reading the book of Job the week Mark died. We had been through a great deal since we moved to Aviano: the fire and months of clean up; Mark's new intense job in a brand new squadron; Mark's master's degree and the partial amputation of Christina's finger. I was feeling tested, and I wanted to see the ways in which Job responded well and learn from things he could have done better.

Job is famous for his patience. I have always wondered why. I would have made him famous for his fierce loyalty to God. Even though he thought God was acting unjustly in punishing him, he recognized God's right to do so. He understood God possessed all power and was free to do whatever He pleased. Job was unwilling to do as his loving wife suggested, *"Curse God and die."* To which Job replied, *"Shall we accept good from God and not trouble?"* (Job 2:9-10) But when we define patience as long-suffering, then Job is definitely patient. He suffered more loss over time than most of us will face in a lifetime.

What a credit to Job to be seen as both long-suffering and fiercely loyal to God! But the truth of the matter is Job did shake his fist at God and request an audience with Him, *"But I desire to speak to the Almighty and to argue my case with God."* (Job 13:3) During this period, while Job was questioning God's righteousness and justice, he also seems to have gone into a deep depression,

97

wishing he had never been born and wanting to die. That is what happens to us when we lose sight of the stalwart, perfect, unchanging character of God. But God enabled Job to recover by reminding Job about Himself. Out of a storm, God answered Job by asking him a few (about seventy) questions about His creation (Job 38-41). Through the rhetorical nature of the questions, God reminds Job of His sovereignty, His omnipresence and His omnipotence. When Job finally understands what God is teaching him from the storm, Job's reply is one of wisdom, full of an awareness of the insignificance of His own plans next to God's:

"Then Job replied to the Lord: 'I know that you can do all things; no plan of yours can be thwarted. You asked, "Who is this that obscures my counsel without knowledge?" Surely I spoke of things I did not understand, things too wonderful for me to know." Job 42:1-3

God's plans are too wonderful for us to know! How exciting to be a part of those plans! I have found that when I take my focus off God, I begin to flounder.

Peter's Example

Peter did the same in Matthew 14 when Jesus came out to the disciples' boat walking on the water. Peter's faith is great: *"Lord, if it's you, tell me to come to you on the water."(Matthew 14:28)* And Peter got out of the boat and walked on the water until he took his eyes off Jesus and focused on the wind around him. Then he began to sink.

This is a beautiful picture of my own life. When I find myself sinking, I am too focused on the situation around me. But when I make the effort to look God in the face, I am reminded that it is His character that stabilizes me and I am unshakeable. Job and Peter and you and I

98

need to keep our focus on who God is. When we lose that focus, we all sink. In God we find the One who has all the answers. We do not need to know them all, but we need to focus on the One who does.

God used Marty's death to impact my life in wonderful ways and He continues to do so. I saw how God used Mark's death to impact his family, friends and acquaintances and still does. God has graciously shown me these things to give me that small glimpse into how He is working in His world. But if He had not shown me these things, I would still have to take on faith that God is at work and He knows what he is doing. His character tells me that. God is at work, implementing His glorious, eternal plan all around us. I want to see as God sees, looking at life through His eyes. Then maybe some day they will inscribe on my tombstone, a line to my favorite Amy Grant song, "She had her Father's eyes."

DESIGNER HANDS

WHAT SEEMS RANDOM,

HAS BEEN FILTERED THROUGH GOD'S PRECISE HAND.

WHAT SEEMS MEANINGLESS,

HAS BEEN STRAINED BY GOD'S PURPOSEFUL FINGERS.

WHAT SEEMS UNFAIR,

HAS BEEN SCREENED BY THE HAND OF THE RIGHTEOUS
    JUDGE.

WHAT SEEMS HEARTLESS,

HAS BEEN CAREFULLY SIFTED BY LOVE'S VERY OWN
    HANDS.

WHEN LIFE SEEMS OUT OF CONTROL,

KNOW THAT WHAT HAS COME IS NO MISTAKE.

IN THE MIDST OF LIFE'S TURMOIL

LOOK FOR THE TOUCH OF THE DESIGNER'S HAND.

JANUARY 2001

Freedom From Rights

I am an American.
I grew up believing I have the right to life, liberty, and the
    pursuit of happiness.
I was taught that no one had a right to violate those basic
    rights of mine.
And I was justified in being angry if anyone infringed on those
    rights.

Then I learned that I am a sinner.
In God's eyes, my payment for those sins is death.
Death is what I'm deserving of, not life, not liberty, not
    happiness.
Death.

Then came Jesus.
He is the only human ever to walk this earth with rights before
    God.
He had the right to be called God's perfect Son, because He
    was sinless.
He alone had the right to live.

But Jesus died.
He willingly gave up His right to life and His power over life for
    me.
He died the gruesome death I deserve for my sin.
He paid for me.

Now I have life, eternal.
It is a gift just like every good thing I have received.
He gives gifts to me out of His abundant grace and mercy.
I deserve none of them.

Each day I have breath;
Each relationship with my family, my friends, and those I love;
Each morsel of food; each dime I own; each day I'm sheltered
        from the cold;
Is but another undeserved gift from God.

I know now I have no rights before God.
So I can be thankful for each good thing God brings in my life.
And when He chooses to take them away,
I can be thankful for the gift while it lasted.

I still have rights as an American.
But through Jesus' blood, God gives me the right to be called
        a child of His.
Life, liberty, and happiness are all fleeting.
The gift of eternal life is forever.

I am finally free from rights.

February 1997

Chapter 7

Expressing Gratitude:
Thank You?

Be joyful always; pray continually; give thanks in all circumstances, for this is God's will for you in Christ Jesus.
I Thessalonians 5:16-18

Valentine's Day – For those of us who are hopeless romantics, the day is either one of the best or one of the worst days of the year. Nineteen days after Mark's death it rolled around. Thankfully, I was still much too busy to spend large amounts of time pondering my loneliness that Valentine's Day. Since Valentine's Day is so much fun for me, I had already bought Mark a few presents that I never had the opportunity to give him. One gift was a personalized plaque about true love. I had that placed in his casket. The other gift was a mug displaying a hand saying "I love you" in sign language. I drank my coffee from that most of the year. But a year later, after making it through that first year without Mark, Valentine's Day loomed like a dark storm cloud. I remember one trip to the mall: teddy bears, red hearts, red lingerie, and the words "I love you" were everywhere I looked.

Looking for Love

It was my first Valentine's Day back in the United States after several years in Europe, so I had forgotten what a big deal we Americans make of that day of love. It felt as though someone had painted the entire mall red just to annoy me and to exacerbate my loneliness. And to make matters worse, it seemed as if I were noticeably the only solo person in the mall that day. Everyone else was walking arm in arm with someone. I can not say I had a thankful attitude as I shuffled through the mall, trying not to make eye contact with anyone. The emotions I was harboring were a combination of intense indignation and loneliness. At least half of those women, I was pretty sure, were not even Christians. Probably half again of those women were not even walking closely with God. And yet God blessed them with someone to love and I had no one. I felt as alone as I ever remember feeling.

I went home and had it out with God. I did not get far before God reminded me of a few passages. One was at the end of the Parable of the Workers in the Vineyard in the book of Matthew. The landowner in the story had hired the first workers early in the morning and agreed to pay them each a denarius. Then throughout the day, the landowner went out at the third, sixth, ninth and eleventh hour of the day to hire more workers. At the end of the day he paid them each a denarius. The first workers grumbled, *"These men who were hired last worked only one hour...and you have made them equal to us who have borne the burden of the work and the heat of the day."* (Matthew 20: 12) The landowner replied, *"Friend, I am not being unfair to you. Didn't you agree to work for a denarius? Take your pay and go. I want to give the man who was hired last the same as I gave you. Don't I have the right to do what I want with my own money? Or are you envious because I am generous?"* (Matthew 20:13-15)

How many times do we decide how fair God is based not on His relationship to us, but on what He chooses to give to others? It is so easy for me to look at what God has given others, especially those who do not love Him, and whine that God is unfair. God, as the landowner in this parable, tells me I have no right to compare what God gives me to what He gives others. Is it not obvious from this parable that those workers who worked only an hour in the fields, yet were paid a day's wage would be drawn to that landowner? I can see them wanting to work hard for Him every day because they were so grateful for His generosity. It is clear in this parable that God loves to give good gifts, and He uses them to draw people to Himself. When I manage to step out of my own pity party, I realize how thankful I should be that God is in hot pursuit of the hearts of the lost. I am glad He is going after the hearts of those I love who do not know Him. If He wants to use a tender romance to draw a lost woman to Him, I need to be thankful He loves her enough to give her that gift.

More Comparisons

The second passage God not-so-coincidentally led me to was the Parable of the Prodigal Son. I had read and heard the story hundreds of times as a child and as many times since, thinking it was merely a sweet story about how God is always waiting for the lost to come to their senses and return to Him. This time, however, God showed me the same story in a different light. God had a great truth to reveal to me at the end of the story through a simple statement from the Father that I had never really noticed. The prodigal son has been wandering for years in the mire of carnality; the Father seems to reward this stray son more than the son who had remained loyal to his father all his life. The loyal, faithful son complains (as I was doing):

"But he answered his father, 'Look! All these years I've been slaving for you and never disobeyed your orders. Yet you

never gave me even a young goat so I could celebrate with my friends. But when this son of yours who has squandered your property with prostitutes comes home, you kill the fatted calf for him!' 'My son,' the father said, ' you are always with me, and everything I have is yours.'" Luke 15:29-31

See how the older son missed it? How could he have missed it? How could I have missed it? We were both so busy playing the comparison game that we lost focus of the most important reward. A joyous feast and a loving husband are wonderful gifts, but they dim in comparison with the honor of having had a close, abiding relationship with the Father. *I have been with God always and everything God has is mine.* How can I look at a wife who has never known the Lord with envy just because she has a husband?

> *"Better is one day in your courts than a thousand elsewhere;*
> *I would rather be a doorkeeper in the house of my God than dwell in the tents of the wicked."*   Psalm 84: 10

I possess the greatest gift ever given: life in sweet intimacy with my God through the blood sacrifice of His perfect Son! Everything God has is mine: His joy, His hope, His strength, His forgiveness, His unconditional love, His grace, His master plan for this world, and His assurance of an eternal life walking the streets of gold with His presence for the light. The glorious riches of God are mine to enjoy. May the Lord find it in His heart to forgive me for envying *anyone* who does not know Him.

"Is the glass half empty or half full?" This has been a question posed to us repeatedly in our lives. How we respond, "half empty" or "half full" is supposed to tell us how we naturally see life, pessimistically or optimistically. The world recently has been telling us that we have a right to a full glass. If we have any less, we are victims of somebody: our parents, our schools, our society, our government, our god or anyone who takes a drop away from our full glass. And guess what? No one has a full glass so we are a society full of victims. We, Christians, have been given a much more powerful platform from which to view life. If there is even a drop in our glass, we have been given something we do not deserve:

"For the wages of sin is death, but the gift of God is eternal life in Christ Jesus our Lord."   Romans 6:23

We deserve death, each of us. So anything we get in our glasses is an unwarranted gift from the Father above who loves to give good gifts. While this outlook may sound melodramatic or self-deprecating, it is actually a powerful viewpoint for a thankful, joyful life. When others are saying, "Woe is me, half my glass has been taken from me." We can say, "Thank you God for giving me even this undeserved refreshment!" And, when God chooses to take it away, we do not hold tightly, for we never deserved the gift. If we can grasp and embrace this one concept, it will revolutionize our lives as Christians. People tell me I deserve a new husband, since I have been faithful to God through the death of my first husband. But I know I have abundantly more now than I deserve, so I hope God does not decide to give me what I deserve!

Our rights have become a stumbling block for powerful Christian living. The citizens of our nation need to have rights so we can remain a civilized nation, and it is our nation's duty to uphold these rights. Paul claimed his rights as a Roman citizen to have fair treatment. But we have somehow extended our civil rights to our relationships with God, thinking we have rights before Him. But God is the only one who really has rights:

"But who are you, O man, to talk back to God? Shall what is formed say to him who formed it, 'Why did you make me like this?' Does not a potter have the right to make out of the same lump of clay some pottery for noble purposes and some for common use?"   *Romans 9:20-21*

We are the lumps of clay. By God's hand we were created for His use. He has all the rights. The only rights we have are those He has graciously chosen to give to us undeserved: the right to a free will; the right to enter into the holy of holies and commune with God directly; the right to be His ambassadors, and the right to be called children of God. But we somehow think we have the right to a smooth life, the right to relationships with people who love us as much as we love them, the right to health, the right to great parents and obedient children. God has given these to other people as gifts so we somehow feel a right to them as well. And we become angry with God when He chooses not to give us one of these gifts or He takes one away. Rather than focus on the gifts with which God has blessed us, it is easy to focus on what He *has not* done. It takes a deliberate act of the will to focus on being thankful for the undeserved gifts in our lives and to let go of the gifts God has taken away or never given us.

Thankfulness is a Choice, not a Feeling

The other night Christina, now seven, called me into her room. "Mom," she said excitedly, "I have thirty-one things I'm thankful for." Then she proceeded to go through a well thought out list of things, "My parents, my grandparents, my brothers, my sister, my house, my bed, my church, my pastor, my school, my teacher, my heart...". I wondered how many of us ever take the time to list all the things we are thankful for, and how many of us could come up with thirty-one things as easily as she did. I realized that thankfulness is a learned way of life. We may naturally look at the glass as half empty, but God says that is not how we are to live; it does not lead to the content, fulfilled lives God wants for us. We have to choose to train our minds to be thankful for the undeserved drops in our glass. *Until we fully grasp we deserve nothing, we will never fully appreciate anything.*

Anniversaries are a wonderful time to choose thankfulness. We can be bitter and think of all that could have been or we can thank God for what was. On the anniversary of Mark's birthday, we decided to celebrate his life on this earth. On the anniversary of his death, we cry as we remember our loss but we celebrate Mark's entry into heaven. On the anniversary of our wedding, I can celebrate a beautiful love and thank God for the opportunity to fulfill my wedding vows.

Those who are not accustomed to living a thankful life may think these ideas are phony or contrived. "I do not feel thankful, so I am not going to insult God by pretending I am." This is a valid argument, and I agree that there is no need to be phony with a God who knows your thoughts. But God says to, "give thanks in all circumstances." How do we rectify our feelings with what

God commands? We have to be forthright with God and work at thankfulness:

"God, I know you tell me to be thankful, but I do not feel thankful. You know that. I want to honor Your Word when it does not seem to make sense only because it is You who said it. Help me to have a thankful heart, Lord. Thank you for the man You brought into my life for me to love for ten years. Thank You for the joy he brought into my life. Thank you that You brought him to me when I had done nothing to deserve his love or Your love. Thank You that I can say our wedding vows were fulfilled; we parted only at death. In a culture steeped in divorce, thank You that he did not leave me, even during the hard times. I am missing him deeply; You know that. Thank you that You understand the depth of my loss and my loneliness, and You are always here to keep me company, to love me, and to care for me."

Thankfulness is not merely what is best for our witness of Christ to others, it is what is best for us. Thankful people look for the gift in every situation, even the tough ones. Pity parties are the opposite of thankfulness. One leads us down the path toward depression, the other the path of joy despite circumstances. The choice is ours.

Thanks Living

Lord, I say, "thank You" all the time.
Yet it often seems so hollow.
Maybe this year I need to say it with my life,
Instead of just my mouth.

To say, "thank You" for the mercy
You have repeatedly shown me,
May I choose to show compassion,
When condemnation is warranted.

To say, "thank You" for the grace
Of Your riches lavished on me,
May I be willing to give to others,
Who can give nothing in return.

To say, "thank You" for Your forgiveness
Of the same old thing again,
May I offer forgiveness and restoration
To any who wrong me.

To say, "thank You" for Your presence
Which fills my life with love,
May I be willing to give of my time
To someone who needs my love.

This year I want to show you
My thankfulness is more than hollow words.
May my life proclaim my gratitude to You.
As I commit myself to thanks living.

Thanksgiving 2000

111

Section Three:

Press In

hermeneutics between the Bible and my life. I have seminary training. Unlike simple people who obey the Bible because they don't realize how complicated it is, I find ambiguity in every verse. I don't obey Scripture, I discuss it.

Patti Broderick and I, at the crossroads of our respective widowhood, evidently heard the same statistics and psychological findings regarding the "natural" course of grief and the amount of time needed to "process" it. I went with the statistics and gave myself permission to be as bad as I wanted to be. She, more simpleminded, files the following report: "So I chose, instead, to bank my life on Scripture being true, and I was not going to let even well-meaning Christians talk me out of it." In this she cites as fixed anchors for the soul such meditations as the following:

"'For I know the plans I have for you,' declares the Lord, 'plans to prosper you and not to harm you, plans to give you hope and a future. Then you will call upon me, and come and pray to me, and I will listen to you. You will seek me and find me when you seek me with all your heart. I will be found by you'" (Jeremiah 29:11-14).

In her simpleminded faith, Patti Broderick decided early on, on the basis of such verses as the one above, that she should make an effort to pray and read the Bible more in order to know God better, blithely unmindful of any problematic taint of legalism in that endeavor. She also studied the lives of Abraham and other Hebrews 11 people and, astoundingly, drew motivation from them to imitate their lives of faith.

That is, Ms. Broderick did the very thing that a Gnostic knows not to do: She took the Bible as practical.

They say "write what you know," and I know widowhood. And I can tell you with assurance that what Patti McCarthy Broderick has done is not natural. The default mode of widowhood is not what she has lived. As the author of this fine book has admitted, she made a conscious choice to trust in God, to take His Word as truth, to see opportunity, and to wear His praises publicly on her lips. And she did not find Him disappointing. —

Simple faith

A widowed writer does something highly unusual: She takes God at His Word | by Andree Seu

There were about five minutes of new widowhood when I grasped that I was now in a special demographic where eyes would be on me watching to see God glorified in my circumstances. There was the blinking of an eye when I saw opportunity—a stage for God's "power in weakness" show, a chance to prove Satan wrong in wagering that God's children serve Him only when they're ahead of the game (Job 1). But then I receded again into the pursuit of minimum Christianity: saved by the blood, but entitled to grouse.

I don't outright grouse, not usually. I am sanctified about it—just a well-placed sigh in certain company, just a being "honest" about loneliness. Or, I say nothing at all, either bad or good. If I have known some private comfort in my prayer closet, I never let on, so nobody ever knows it. There's a lyric in the songs my mother used to play in the Frank Sinatra-Robert Goulet 33 LP pity-party days that said something like "happy to be miserable over you." This is the idea.

Now I have received a book in the mail by a widow writing on widowhood: He Said, "Press," by Patti McCarthy Broderick. Let me say that I never read books about widowhood or the Christian life by people whose day job is housewife. I like books by lettered authors with titles like The Twentieth Century or Postmodernism. Leave me alone with my personal life. Let's talk epic themes. But I promised I would read it so I did.

Gnosticism is thought to be a dead church issue: A clique of second- to fourth-century guys thought the writings of Paul were quaint, and good enough for the Christian rabble, but for themselves were superseded by a secret inside track to God through mystical channels far more sophisticated than obedience to Christ's simple commands.

Patti Broderick has written a very simple book about her journey. She cites verses like the following and makes much of them:

"I know that You can do all things . . ." (Job 42:2). "Consider how the lilies grow . . ." (Luke 12:27-28). "This happened that we might not rely on ourselves but on God . . ." (2 Corinthians 1:9). "His divine power has given us everything we need for life and godliness . . ." (2 Peter 1:3).

Ms. Broderick figures that when the Bible says "suffering produces character and character, hope," it means that suffering produces character and character, hope. I, on the other hand, have interposed a baroque system of

Come Unto Me

Lord, You made me with these human emotions,
Yet it seems like You don't want me to have them.

You say, "Do not be anxious about anything."
Yet time after time You put me in circumstances
Which are out of my control,
And anxiety arises inside me before I know it.

You tell me, "Do not fear."
Yet life itself is teeming with situations
Which are much bigger than I am,
And fear uncontrollably wells up inside of me.

You have said, "I will never leave you."
Yet You often remove my friends from me
When I need a friend the most,
And loneliness involuntarily engulfs my soul.

But You also say "Come unto Me."
So out of desperation, I come.

When life spins out of control and anxiety builds,
I see that the Prince of Peace, who has it all under control,
Is beckoning me to fellowship with Him.
Anxiety is a method You use to call me to Yourself.

When fears mount as the future seems perilously uncertain,
I realize that a God who is much bigger than my fears
Is entreating me to sit at His feet.
Fear is Your way of summoning me to seek Your face.

When loneliness looms as You remove my trustworthy friends,
I know the One who sticks closer than a brother,
Is offering His loyal friendship to me.
Loneliness is a sweet reminder that You want to be my best
    friend.

Thank you, Lord, that you give me these emotions,
Hand written invitations to come unto You.

August 2000

Chapter 8

Full Court Press:
Persevering

"Even youths grow tired and weary, and young men stumble and fall; but those who hope in the Lord will renew their strength. They will soar on wings like eagles; they will run and not grow weary, they will walk and not be faint."

Isaiah 40:30-31

One night I was packing lunches for school after the children had gone to bed. I was cutting up an apple and the knife slipped, slicing a deep gash in my hand. As I held pressure on my wound, I grew light headed and felt as though I would pass out. I pictured the children waking up in the morning to find their mother had bled to death on the kitchen floor. Times like those I felt so alone, and the light at the end of the tunnel sure appeared to be making train noises.

The perpetual aloneness seemed to drain me like a car battery with the headlights left on. Weeks turned into months; months turned into years and I was still widowed with young children who were growing up without a father. I realized at one point that David and Christina had lived more life without a dad than they had with, and Bryan was rapidly approaching that point as well. I will be the first to admit single parenting is physically tiring, but the aloneness is even more exhausting. I bought a plaque and put it in my kitchen that read, "I am woman. I am invincible. I am tired." There were times when life seemed more of a "survival of the fittest" rather than that promised "joyful journey."

My life reminded me of marathons I have run. In this 26.2-mile race, even those in the greatest of shape get tired because the race is *just long*. Runners typically hit "the wall' somewhere near the 20 mile point and they do not feel they can go on. I experienced "the wall" over and over again in the years following Mark's death. There were days when I would have paid big money for a second set of hands to just pick up after those children and share the emotional burden. Occasionally, I would raise my fist to God and cry out, "Why didn't You take me?" Looking back, I can see that when the days were long and I was emotionally and physically spent, what I was desperately searching for was a glimmer of hope so that I might stay the course. My mouth was parched, and I just need to know that a dribble of water could possibly be on my tongue some time soon.

"Therefore since we have been justified through faith, we have peace with God through our Lord Jesus Christ, through whom we have gained access by faith into this grace in which we now stand. And we rejoice in the hope of the glory of God. Not only so, but we also rejoice in our sufferings, because we know that suffering produces perseverance; perseverance, character; and character, hope. And hope does not disappoint us, because God has poured out his love into our hearts by the Holy Spirit, whom he has given us." Romans 5:1-5

Hope is the energy source of the human soul. We hit "the wall" emotionally without it. Where did this widow find hope for her soul during those seemingly hopeless days? First and foremost, we are anchored by our eternal hope of being given the privilege of being partakers of the glory of God. We will one day walk with God, unfettered by this flesh. We will be free to grasp God in His splendor and delight. I believe we were designed to long for that life. Our earthly struggles are reminders to us that there is something much better. Regardless of what this world takes from us, it cannot take away that hope. That is dependent on God and God is completely dependable.

But what about hope for the every day, knowing that it may be quite some time before we enter our eternal rest? In the Romans passage above, God says we can rejoice in our suffering because of who we can become through it. "Suffering produces perseverance," we know instinctively because when we suffer we either persevere or we faint, lose heart, and give up. Most of us probably waffle back and forth between the two when we suffer. But if we can persevere through God's strength, then God develops character in us. It is then through our God-matured character that we can see hope in even the gloomiest of situations. But character does not just happen. It takes work and submission to God, the Master Character-Builder.

Building Up Endurance

When I was in the military, we had to run a timed 1-1/2 miles each year in order to show that we were keeping ourselves in shape. I am a medium-framed woman with no incredible gift of swiftness or endurance. But I have run faithfully, three to five miles most every day since I was 13 years old. So a 1-1/2 mile run is no trouble. Our whole squadron met at the track, decked out in running attire to run together. I was out there with the young 18 and 19-year-old airmen in the squadron. They were strapping men still in their youth. The race would be your classic "Tortoise and the Hare" run.

They sprinted around the track the first lap or two, then slowed greatly, and by the last few laps, they were walking, panting and sometimes vomiting at the finish line. I usually finished well ahead of them and had my breath back soon after the run. They would always come up and say, "But Ma'am, it's not fair; of course you won, you're a runner." Then I would say, "Look at me and look at yourself and tell me what makes me a runner. It certainly is not that I have an edge over you with my physical stature. What makes me a runner is I get up every morning and I run."

After saying this year after year to these young men, I realized I was doing the same thing with my own spiritual life. I would look up to a godly woman and I would say, "But God, it is not fair, she is just godly," as if there were some "spiritual gene" that God had forgotten to give me. But over time, He showed me the truth; *godly women become godly by spending time with God, every day.* It is not a wonder that my reactions and attitudes are not godly if I am not spending time with God. My reactions and attitudes, without constant shaping and molding by God, are just like the race those young men ran, untrained, unequipped, and desperately unready. They ran with no strategy, and the result was they lost the race and became physically ill. I had been trying to run my spiritual life as they ran that race. When I really needed it, I tried to be godly, but I did not know God. I could not fake it, just like those men could not fake being runners.

Spiritual Meanders

When we are not determined to grow spiritually, we often take "detours" in our spiritual lives to "find ourselves." When we come up against circumstances that try our spiritual commitment, we find ourselves to be not as committed as we thought we were. So we float along in life, sometimes allowing our spiritual lives to be rejuvenated by a retreat or a speaker, only to relapse into our previous, powerless faith. We are at a point in life where we are trying to determine the most important aspect of who we are, our character, and by neglect we allow our circumstances and our relationships to shape that.

When we allow our circumstances to determine who we are, then years from now, we will look ourselves in the mirror and we will not like the person we have become, nor will our lives have been honoring to God. We must first determine who God would have us to be, and then set our paths deliberately on that course.

A Deliberate Course

I can become a godly woman by spending time with God. I can become a prayer warrior by spending time in prayer. I can become a woman of stalwart integrity by making every word that comes out of my mouth true. I can bring glory to God with my life by submitting my will to God's. What kind of person God wants me to be is clear in scripture. *If we have no character goals, we will end up with no character.* Jesus said, *"Be perfect, therefore, as your heavenly Father is perfect."* *(Matthew 5:48)*. None of us is there yet, so until the day Jesus comes to take us home with Him, we ought to be constantly allowing God to mold

121

our character to be in line with His Son's. One of God's favorite teaching tools is our suffering.

In this independent, stubborn woman's life, God has tenderly allowed the carpet to be pulled out from beneath my feet to get me looking up. He has used these trials to shape my character. My definition of a maturing character is one who is in the process of replacing his will with the will of the Father. A maturing character is becoming more like Jesus, who said, *"The one who sent me is with me; he has not left me alone, for I always do what pleases him."* *(John 8:29)* I can rejoice in my suffering then when I can look expectantly at how God will mature my character to become more like Jesus. This brings me hope now on this earth: hope that I will be used by God to further His purposes; hope that the reflection of the Holy Spirit in me is clearer each day; hope that I will continue to relinquish more control with each trial so God can work His master plan in and through my life. *"And hope does not disappoint us..." Romans 5:5*

Handling Real Emotions

No matter how mature the Christian, there is always a struggle with emotions. We are lonely. Anxieties entrap us. Fears come and go. The "joyful journey" is filled with emotions we are admonished in God's Word not to have. Here God presents Himself as the answer to our emotions:

"Do not be anxious about anything...but ...present your requests to God." *Philippians 4:6*

"There is no fear in love...but...perfect love drives out fear." *I John 4:18*

122

"Even youths grow tired and weary, and young men stumble and fall... but... those who hope in the Lord will renew their strength."   *Isaiah 40:30-31*

God created us to have emotions. It does us no good to pretend they do not exist. I have fought against and suppressed my emotions, but that never seemed to help. They were always there, ready to rear their ugly heads at a less-than-opportune time, and usually with greater intensity. So it was a real revelation to me finally to understand that **my emotions are handwritten invitations from God.** God wants me to come to Him when my emotions are out of control because He is the only One who truly understands and He is always in control. My emotions were created to draw me to the One who has the big picture, to lead me to sit at His feet and find refuge in His secure arms. Only at His feet can the senseless make sense. Only in His hands can we find peace in the midst of a storm. Only close to Him does this life have meaning.

Refreshment from the Body of Christ

God is a wonderful Counselor for our emotions and The Source of spiritual truth. If you read God's Word, it becomes evident that He does not stop there. He is also concerned about the physical well being of the widow, the orphan and any other down trodden soul. How does God provide physical aid to the parched soul? The body of Christ is teeming with living water waiting to be guzzled. For me, this meant I had to swallow some of that ugly wad of unproductive pride I carry around like a lead weight so my pallet would be free to savor that refreshing Living Water.

123

"Come to me, all you who are weary and burdened, and I will give you rest. Take my yoke upon you and learn from me, for I am gentle and humble in heart, and you will find rest for your souls. For my yoke is easy and my burden is light."
Matthew 11:28-30

"Come unto me," Jesus says to those of us who labor, who are heavy laden, or whose burden seems too great to bear. I think this would include the entire population on this earth but definitely the smaller population of the grieving. Because Jesus is so big, there are many ways to come unto Him, but each of them requires that we learn from Him and follow His example of humility. "Coming unto Jesus" requires first admitting we have a need that we are unable to fulfill by ourselves. It was so hard for me to learn I could call on a friend for help. I think of the joy I robbed from my friends when I recall all the times I gritted my teeth and hung onto that lead weight rather than admitting my need.

My pride said I could be everything my children and I needed; my common sense told me otherwise. There were two choices before me: I could let my children's needs go unmet, or I could swallow that ugly pride and find help in the church body. I soon learned that this is one of the ways God could be my husband and my children's Father, through His body, the church. Some of the emotional and physical needs we had were real and God was able physically to meet those needs with His church.

As I learned to swallow my pride, God became more real to me in the physical ways He took care of me. The times that I did reach out for help, the body was incredibly responsive. Many times I called a girlfriend, just needing someone to talk to and she would drop her plans to meet my three little ones and me at the local bagel shop for lunch. I could use some tools around the house, but I called on my father-in-law for many of the handyman chores. I kept a running "Daddy-do" list around the house. I had my father fly in from Virginia for some of the bigger construction jobs around the house. I called the church when I had a flat tire and the youth pastor showed up to change my tire.

I relied on these men and others from the church for romping time with the boys. They loved to wrestle and I do not. Some college-aged men at church were more than happy to fill this wrestling need for the boys, and they gleaned some parenting hints in the process. When the children were too young to be left alone in the house, I had trouble finding a way to get in my daily run. A family with two home-schooled teenagers heard of my need and took turns with their mother, coming every morning at 6:00 AM so I could run before the children arose for the day. The Cain Family would never accept money even though the father was between jobs because they wanted to do it as a ministry. God showed me His heart in beautiful ways through the Cain Family and His church body.

More Waiting

The Christian walk is in many respects an endurance race. We have no idea how long we will be in the race. It could end tomorrow or we could live to be old and frail. It is up to us to be ready for either. Life as a young widow is much the same. I have to pace myself, knowing that this may be my enduring lot in life, and if God chooses to change my status, that is His prerogative alone. One thing I was keenly aware of was my desire to

125

be remarried again some day. I would have made that day much sooner if I had been in charge instead of God. The dating scene was indeed a pressure cooker. Kind-hearted friends set me up with Christian men. I went out with some wonderful men. I even fell in love one time. But nothing seemed to turn out to be *it*. There were a few things I was sure of that I had not grasped when I was a baby Christian on the dating scene the first time.

Marriage was instituted by God to draw us closer to God. I would only marry if having that man in my life would help me grow in Christ and his having me in his life would benefit his growth in Christ. The first time around I was looking for someone to fulfill my needs. This time I understood no man could fulfill all my needs; only God could do that. Marriage then would be an option for me only if we could accept each other's weaknesses and help each other become more like Christ. I began praying for *God's man in God's timing for God's purposes*. There was a freedom in this prayer for I understood that, even if everything seemed perfect to me, the man I thought was the right one might not be the one God had chosen for me, or perhaps it was not God's timing.

While the loneliness and the desire were real, the waiting was bearable, because I trusted God to do what He knew was best. There is some excitement in waiting on an unpredictable God. When we really trust that He is working things out for good, it is much easier to listen and wait with anticipation. The disappointments are still real, but there is a sense of joy in understanding that He is able to use even disappointments for His purposes. He is faithfully molding me into the image of His Son, perhaps preparing me to some day be the wife He wants me to be.

Consider it pure joy, my brothers, whenever you face trials of many kinds, because you know that the testing of your faith develops perseverance. Perseverance must finish its work so that you may be mature and complete, not lacking anything."
                                                                James 1:2-4

It is good to know that God is not limited to just one playing field. He is always working His will so that His name might be known and His love spread throughout the world. That is the big umbrella in life under which God operates. At the same time He is working on drawing each of us, individually unto Him to allow us to become "mature and complete, not lacking anything." We must persevere so that God can finish His work in and through us. Then we will be able to say along with the Apostle Paul:

I have fought the good fight, I have finished the race, I have kept the faith. Now there is in store for me the crown of righteousness, which the Lord, the righteous Judge will award to me on that day – and not only to me but also to all who have longed for his appearing.   II Timothy 4:7-8

As I walk along the beach,
My foot leaves an imprint,
An indentation deep in the sand.
I feel like I'm changing the world.
Making a difference.
Then the waves come in
And wipe out the footprint
Leaving no sign it was ever there.
It reminds me of my life,
Devoid of lasting impact,
Washed out in a sea of humanity,
Unnoticed over time.
Then You gently remind me
That You are the source of the waves.
They don't wash aimlessly about
And die on the shore,
But each wave has meaning
Moving sand little by little
Where You want it to go.
And I have helped You
With my single footprint,
To accomplish Your purposes.
You don't ask me to build sand bars,
Or relocate entire beaches.
You simply ask me to be willing
To leave a footprint,
One step at a time.

August 2003

Reflections of the Son

Many mornings I arise early to watch the sunrise.
Each sunrise is wholly unique, a new experience.
On clear, crisp, cloudless mornings,
The sunrise is disappointingly brief and anticlimactic.
But on days when dramatic clouds stretch across the
sky,
Neon colors seem to light the heavens on fire.
Our lives are like the sky at sunrise;
For our beauty is merely a reflection of the Son.
On days when life is smooth sailing, with no clouds in
sight,
The world has little opportunity to notice the Son in us.
But when our lives are splattered with rough stormy
clouds,
The Son's brilliant radiance can shine with boldness.
We can't let the clouds of life overtake us,
And shut out the light of the Son.
For then we have no light by which to walk,
And our lives cannot display the Son's splendor.
But the clouds of our lives can be seen as the canvas
On which God can paint a beautiful sunrise;
A scene so breathtaking, the world can't help but look
up
And marvel at the sheer brilliance of the Artist.
Then the same clouds which might have weighed us
down
Become opportunities for us to reflect the Son.
What an honor it is when God puts clouds in our lives
So that others may behold His majesty.

Spring 1996

Chapter 9

God's Press Corps:
Giving Glory to God

"As he went along, he saw a man blind from birth. His disciples asked him, 'Rabbi, who sinned, this man or his parents, that he was born blind?' 'Neither this man nor his parents sinned,' said Jesus, 'but this happened so that the work of God might be displayed in his life.'" John 9:1-3

One night I had a dream. I dreamt that Satan was roaming about the earth and came to present himself to God. The Lord said to Satan, "Have you considered my servant, Patti? She is faithful to me." And Satan said, "Of course she is faithful, you have given her that wonderful, supportive husband. But remove him from her and she will curse you to your face." The Lord replied, "If her husband is taken from her, you will see, she will be faithful to me and continue to bring me glory."

Okay, so it was actually more of a daydream than a real dream, but it brought me so much hope. As I said earlier, I was reading the book of Job the week Mark died. I have always been struck by God's confidence in Job's faithfulness. God knew that Job's heart was His, unconditionally. There were no circumstances that would cause Job to renounce his God. Murderous thieves stole his livelihood and killed all of his servants; natural disasters took the lives of still more livestock, his servants, and his seven sons and three daughters; and finally Job was covered from head to foot with painful sores. *And Job worshipped God and did not sin in what he said.* What would cause a man to have such fierce loyalty? He must have known and trusted God implicitly despite the pain in his heart and the physical pain he endured.

Of course, it is quite a presumptuous stretch to replace Job's name with mine. Still, it was encouraging to me that God might trust my heart enough to put me through a small trial, knowing I would remain faithful to him. It was heartening to me that God could use my plight as He did Job's to bring Himself glory in some way. And presumptuous or not, I was going to show God He did well in trusting me.

The Uninvited Platform

It was evident to me from the moment of Mark's death that all eyes were on me. How would this Jesus freak respond to God handing her this tragedy? What difference does her faith make? Is she in denial? When will the finality of her loss hit her? What would I do if I were the one widowed? How would I survive? I knew these thoughts were on the minds of those watching both close up and from a distance. God had given me a platform to use for His glory, and I wanted to just be faithful to His calling.

The platform began with the notification of Mark's death and continued for years. The large group of colonels and their wives that was convened to give me the news was attentive. The friends and family who had gathered were watching. The attendees at the memorial service and the funeral gave me a respectful stage to pontificate about my faith and my loss. Then in our new home, our new neighborhood, our new church, our new schools, people were shocked to hear of our loss and open to hearing of our sustaining faith. During an era full of uncertainties and questions, the platform God had given me was as undeniable as it was uncomfortable. But I believe sincerely that it was also an honor.

Perfection Through Weakness

Most of us facing tragedy do not think of it as an honor. I think of Marty Staton's parents. I am sure they would much rather have had their son alive than face the "honor" of a platform because of his death. This is true for all of us who face tragedy, I am sure. But if tragedies do occur in this sinful world, and they do, then what do we do when it strikes home? We sink our anchors deep in the only Rock we know is strong enough to hold us through the storms, God. We pray faithfully and earnestly that God might use us for His glory despite our confusion. We remind ourselves that it is indeed an honor that God would choose to use us for His higher purposes. And we rest, as Paul managed to do in our weaknesses:

"But he said to me, "My grace is sufficient for you, for my power is made perfect in weakness." Therefore I will boast all the more gladly about my weaknesses, so that Christ's power may rest on me. That is why, for Christ's sake, I delight in weaknesses, in insults, in hardships, in persecutions, in difficulties. For when I am weak, then I am strong."
II Corinthians 12:9-10

What are we to make of these verses? Paul had a "thorn in his flesh," "a messenger of Satan to torment him." Yet he managed to find in the midst of his personal weakness an arena to display the humbling powers of God. Would Paul have preferred to have God remove that thorn? Yes. Paul pleaded with God three times to remove that thorn. But God replied that He needed Paul in that weakened state to be a vessel of God's strength. The supernatural strength

133

God gives us to endure hardship is more evident when our own strength is gone. Then there is no question as to the source of the strength. The morning of the memorial service in Aviano, I felt God's strength in physical ways. I had my back-up speaker lined up to speak for me should I not have the strength to talk. But I sensed as I looked up at those massive mountains on the Italian-Austrian border, which God spoke into being, that God's strength would shine through my weakness. People had to know I could barely stand. I even had Dad McCarthy escort me so I would not fall. But the power God gave me to speak boldly on His behalf came directly from God's hand, for I had no such power in myself. I pray it was as obvious to the crowd as it was to me.

In many other ways, God displayed His strength through our weaknesses. The children adjusted well and I found joy, hope and peace by sitting faithfully at the feet of the Source of joy, hope and peace. People often commented that I must be a "strong woman" to do as well as I was doing with the children and for myself. I found I began to enjoy receiving that compliment and savored it whenever it came my way. Then God brought me to the story of Peter's denials of Jesus. He made it clear to me that I, just like Peter, had been denying Jesus. When complimented as a strong woman, I would just say humbly, "Thank you."

Acknowledging the Source

Only after rereading Peter's story did I realize that in saying nothing about my source of strength, the cock was crowing:

"Immediately a rooster crowed. Then Peter remembered the word Jesus had spoken: 'Before the rooster crows, you will disown me three times.' And he went outside and wept bitterly."
Matthew 26:75

I knew exactly why the children had adjusted well and why I had a hopeful outlook, but by failing to reveal my Source of strength, I was claiming the power for myself. And the rooster crowed, time after time. I began calling that crowing sound that would go off in my head when I had denied Christ by omission my "Peter Alert." My Peter Alert prompted me to speak out when it would have been easier not to speak. Moses did not enter the Promised Land because he claimed God's power for himself. An ambassador would be fired quickly if he began pretending to be the President. Likewise, I can not be part of an effective press corps for God if I keep claiming His powers are mine. Thankfully, God has been patient and merciful with me as I attempt to get out of the way and give God the glory due Him.

Comforting the Grieving

Unfortunately, Mark is not the only military pilot to die for his country. Many young widows and children have been left. I have met young men and women widowed by cancer, rock climbing accidents, car accidents, heart attacks, suicide and farm accidents. For a young woman who knew only one widow under 60 before Mark's death, the number of young widows and widowers I met after his death has been overwhelming. Since I do not believe in coincidences, I was sure God had a message for me in the sheer number of widows and widowers He was bringing into my life. God's word confirmed it:

135

"Now that I, your Lord and Teacher, have washed your feet, you also should wash one another's feet. I have set you an example that you should do as I have done for you."

John 13:14

"Praise be to the God and Father of our Lord Jesus Christ, the Father of compassion and the God of all comfort, who comforts us in all our troubles, so that we can comfort those in any trouble with the comfort we ourselves have received."

II Corinthians 1:3-4

It could not be much clearer than that. God has been bringing all these young widows and widowers into my life for a reason, that I might serve them, and comfort them with the comfort God has given me. The God of all comfort is inviting me to join Him in His work on the missionary field with Him right here in my own back yard. As you have read in the pages of this book, God has brought me comfort through the hope in His Word, through the helping hands of His body of believers, and especially through the ways He met me as I have sought Him. What kind of ambassador would I be if I did not share these truths with others who are hurting and in need of the same kind of comfort? As you might guess, I am writing this book because of this conviction. But in earlier years I used much more simple forms of offering comfort. Notes, verses, phone calls, invitations to coffee or dinner are all ways we can offer truth, while letting someone know we understand and care.

Perhaps it was God's fulfillment of His promise that changed my view of God and my part in His eternal plan forever:

> *You will seek me and find me when you seek me with all your heart. I will be found by you.*   Jeremiah 29:13-14

I did seek God hard following Mark's death. There was no book I could read during those early days other than the Bible. As years passed I was also challenged by Oswald Chambers' My Utmost for His Highest (Barbour, 1963):

"Whenever the insistence is in the point that God answers prayer, we are off the track. The meaning of prayer is that we get hold of God, not of the answer."

This convicted me that I ought to be seeking the face and not merely the hand of God. When my children butter me up because they want something and then smother me with gushing praise because I have given them something, their "I love you, Mom" rings insincere. Likewise, when they are disciplined and lash out in anger they fail to see the pain and deep love written all over my face. In each of these cases, they think they are relating to me but really they are just responding to the "hand of Mom," which sometimes they really like and sometimes they hate. But when a child of mine, unprompted, snuggles up with me on the couch, looks up into my eyes and whispers, "I love you, Mom. Tell me about your day," then that could be construed as genuine love and an earnest desire to get to know "the face of Mom." It is much the same way with our relationship with God. No wonder our relationship with God is a roller coaster when we look to His hand for the relationship. *The hand of God is mighty, swift and worthy of respect, but not until we look at the face of God are we humbled enough to understand the honor that is due Him.*

Only at His feet, gazing at His perfect holiness and righteousness, do we see how unworthy we even are to be in His presence. Only there can we catch the vision of what an honor it is that He bothers with us, and it is unfathomable that He might want to use us as a vessel for His purposes. Looking into His perfect face, we grasp the truth that God does not need us. Gazing into God's face does for me what chasing the favor of His hand never has; it ignites a burning flame of desire in my soul to live my life bringing Him the glory He deserves. We witness to others of His good news because we love them, because they need Him, but mostly so that God might be given the glory He is due.

We Are God's Canvas

Gazing into God's face has other consequences as well. When we grasp a small portion of His pure holiness, the filth of our own souls is illuminated. The necessity of God doing the work through us rather than us doing work for God becomes glaring:

"I have been crucified with Christ and I no longer live, but Christ lives in me. The life I live in the body, I live by faith in the Son of God, who loved me and gave himself for me."
Galatians 2:20

Everything good that comes from my heart is of God. The value I have is that God formed me especially for His purposes in the image of Himself. When He fills me and

138

works through me, amazing things can happen through me. When I am walking in my flesh, it is amazing the beautiful things I can ruin. God is fulfilling His purposes with or without me. One thing is certain: I want to get my flesh out of the way so God can use me to do the things for which I was designed. If someday you happen upon an invisible woman spouting "Amen," I will have reached my goal:

"For no matter how many promises God has made, they are "Yes!" in Christ. And so through him the "Amen" is spoken by us to the glory of God" II Corinthians 1:20

God is doing the work through me as I gain strength by pressing into Him and believing His promises. The work is His and our lives speak the "Amen" as his promises are fulfilled.

A friend sent me the following verses after the memorial service in Aviano. She said she could see the crown of beauty instead of ashes as I spoke:

"The Spirit of the Sovereign Lord is on me, because the Lord has anointed me to preach the good news to the poor.

He has sent me to bind up the brokenhearted, to proclaim freedom for the captives and release from darkness for the prisoners,

To proclaim the year of our Lord's favor and the day of vengeance of our God

To comfort all who mourn, and provide for those who grieve in Zion

To bestow on them a crown of beauty instead of ashes,

The oil of gladness instead of mourning,

And a garment of praise instead of a spirit of despair.

They will be called oaks of righteousness, a planting of the Lord for the display of his splendor.

Isaiah 61:1-3

Jesus fulfilled these verses in His coming and He is now using us to continue fulfilling these verses. What an honor that God would count me worthy to be used in any way for the display of His splendor!

Face Down

A broken spirit and a contrite heart
*   are what You desire most from me.*

All the service I can offer You;
All the boldness I have for You;
All the love I have for others;
All the words of praise and worship;

All mean nothing before You,
*   without a broken spirit.*

While I think I am someone before You,
*   none of my thoughts and ways can please You.*

Break my heart so I can clearly see
*   the blackness of who I am without You.*

Replace my proud, arrogant heart
*   with Your humble servant heart.*

Fashion my every word and action
*   to reflect the grace and mercy You have shown me.*

For only when I understand I am expendable
*   Can I become invaluable for You.*

And only face down before You
*   Can I hope to rise up to serve You.*

April 1997

141

My Daddy's Lap

"Hey Peanut, come over here,"
I heard my Daddy say.
I ran and jumped in His lap.
His arms felt strong around me.
I gazed into His familiar face.
His eyes burned with love for me.
"Daddy," I said, "Tell me again how much You love me."
Daddy paused and smiled His biggest smile.
"Anytime, Peanut."
"I loved you before you were a peanut."
He stroked my hair gently as He spoke.
"I know you better than anyone else does
And I love you just because you're you."
"You mess up and disobey me sometimes."
"At times you're so stubborn you won't even listen to me."
"But when you find your way back to me,
I can't wait to forgive you."
He spread His arms and showed me the universe.
"My love for you is bigger than all this."
He scooped up the stars in one hand.
"These are beautiful but they mean nothing to me next to you."
"If you ever wonder how much I love you,
Come and sit on my lap.
I'll hold you and tell you as often as you need to hear it."
With that he hugged me warmly and sent me off to play.
But whenever I looked back,
My Heavenly Father's loving eyes were on me,
Caring about each effort I made, each thought I had,
Each wound I endured, each failure and victory in my life.
Loving me as only my Daddy could do.

July 2001

Chapter 10

Wine Press:
Savor the Season

"In this you greatly rejoice, though now for a little while you may have to suffer grief in all kinds of trials. These have come so that your faith- of greater worth than gold, which perishes even though refined by fire- may be proved genuine and may result in praise, glory and honor when Jesus Christ is revealed."

I Peter 1:6-7

When I was thirteen years old, I began running with my Dad. I would like to say I was a great runner and running always came naturally to me. But such was not the case. Running was just part of my heritage passed on to me as routine part of daily living, just like brushing my teeth. My father had run as long as I could remember. While I primarily took up distance running with my father to get into shape for the sports I played, our runs together have turned out to be some of my sweetest memories from my teen years. My father was in many ways what you would expect in an Army colonel: he was strong, decisive, and had high expectations of his followers.

As well as respecting him immensely, I have always enjoyed a close, loving relationship with him. That relationship had a chance to grow deeper on our runs together. Since we talked the whole way, our discussions took our minds off our lungs and legs, and I soon learned to look forward to running with him. Sometimes, the conversations were no deeper than surface level, but often we shared our thoughts on more in-depth religious or philosophical topics. During the summer when most teens were sleeping in until noon, I awoke to run with my Dad. He would softly whistle reveille to rouse me at 5:30 and off we would go. After the run, I would come home, eat breakfast with Dad, and then go back to bed when Dad left for work. That is how much I enjoyed being with my father. They were not long periods of quality time, but they were consistent. With five siblings, it was sweet to get my need for "Daddy time" filled regularly. Looking back on that, I realize my father was wise to give me that time. Through stories, jokes and deep probing questions, he was pointing me in the direction of becoming a responsible young adult. It was during those alone times, those grueling work outs that we came to know each other and my Dad prepared me as best as he could for the things that lay ahead.

A Bond with my Heavenly Father

I can not say I enjoy the act of running in itself, but the benefits that come from it both physically, emotionally and more recently spiritually make it worthwhile. If you add to those benefits the sweet bond I was able to cement with my Dad by enduring long runs through the mud and the elements together, then the pain of running somehow becomes bearable, even desirable. I liken that to my time as a widow and my relationship with God. I surely do not enjoy being a widow. It is certainly not what I would have chosen for myself. But I can see how God is using this time with Him to draw me into a closer love relationship with Him. The sweet bond I am forging with my Heavenly Father by enduring this trial in intimate communion with Him is worth every bit of the heartache. I do not know if I would have ever learned to press so hard into God if I not become a widow. I do believe that it would have taken a long time for me to reach the level of trust I now have with God.

After two years of widowhood, I felt certain God was going to bring me a man any moment to end my widowhood. He is, after all, a good God who loves to give good gifts. I was feeling pretty certain that I had learned all the lessons God had for me from my widowhood, and I was ready to move on to the next phase of life. One thing I have learned from my arrogance is that, when I am sure that I have learned all the lessons God has for me from a situation, that is when He delights in surprising me with more lessons. Such was the case this time. I was sure, I informed God, that I do not have the gift of singleness. During the time of my pronouncement to God I was leading a Bible study in the book of Luke which covered the Parable of the Good Samaritan and was struck by Jesus' ability to turn the questions asked of Him completely upside down.

The Gift of Singleness

Jesus was talking to an expert in the law. The law, he admitted to Jesus, says to, *"love your neighbor as yourself."* In order to justify himself, the expert then asked Jesus, *"Who is my neighbor?"* which could be restated simply as, "Who am I required to love as much as I love myself?" In Jesus' reply, He did as many great teachers do, He answered a question with a question. And in the question He posed, Jesus turned the original question on its head when He asked, basically, "Whom can you find to love?" We fallen beings spend so much of our time looking for the minimum level that is acceptable to God and He, in turn, asks for everything. Is it not just like God

145

to convict me with a parable that seemed to be completely unrelated to my own situation?

When I turned Jesus line of reasoning on the question I had posed to God, "Who has the gift of singleness," or more honestly translated, "How long must I remain single," the response I received from Jesus is a question turned upside down, "How can you see singleness as a gift," or "Who can savor time alone with Me?" Jesus' capsized style of responding makes it clear to me that *God would have me do more than endure my widowhood, He would have me embrace it.* We have been given what seems like rotten grapes and God wants to use us to make fine wine.

"An unmarried woman or virgin is concerned about the Lord's affairs: Her aim is to be devoted to the Lord in both body and spirit. But a married woman is concerned about the affairs of this world- how she can please her husband. I am saying this for your own good, not to restrict you, but that you may live in a right way in undivided devotion to the Lord."

I Corinthians 7:34-35

We do not want to hear this from Paul. But listen closely to what he says and there is a great amount of wisdom in these verses. First of all, we are not being restricted from marrying again; rather we are being reminded that this period of time is special. I will be the first to agree with Paul that, when I was married, I was tied to pleasing my husband. That is as it should be. If God brings me someone to marry again, I will again be tied to pleasing my husband again. The wisdom we can glean from these verses is that right now, as a widow, I am free from the concerns which marriage brings. I can focus during this time, as I was unable to do while married, to undivided devotion to the Lord. It is a precious time, and I do not want to waste it. I want to grow to be so intimately familiar with God that I am a radically different person, wholly devoted to doing and being God's woman. This time is like a desert experience in which the opportunities for the oneness to grow between the Father and me are unbounded.

A Fertile Desert

Jesus was no stranger to desert experiences. He purposefully went to the desert for forty days and forty nights and fasted while being attacked by the tempter. All this He did to allow the Father to prepare Him for the mission the Father was sending Him on. My lot seems rather cushy next to Jesus' desert experience. Jesus used that hard, physically, emotionally and spiritually challenging desert experience to commune with the Father. He allowed His loneliness to drive Him closer to the Father to be strengthened and readied for the ministry before Him. How much more preparation time do I need to become the woman He would have me be? The time I spend alone now with God is teaching me to depend on God and His strength rather than my own. His timing is perfect to strengthen me to do whatever work He calls me to.

"And we rejoice in the hope of the glory of God. Not only so, but we also rejoice in our sufferings, because we know that suffering produces perseverance; perseverance, character; and character, hope. And hope does not disappoint us because God has poured out his love into our hearts by the Holy Spirit, whom he has given us."

Romans 5:3-5

Here is another one of those verses written by Paul that we like to ignore. Who really *"rejoices in their sufferings,"* after all? I think Paul was saying that we do not rejoice in suffering because it is fun; we rejoice in suffering because of what it can produce in us: perseverance, character, and hope. We have already discussed how important hope is to the human spirit. Anyone who has suffered a loss knows how important hope is. But how does suffering produce hope? It seems to me, that as we step out in faith and persevere, as we take God at his Word and press through the difficult times, character development is a natural result. Our hope flourishes as we see that our faithfulness to God has paid off, that God is perfectly faithful to His Word. This is the most exciting part of suffering for me. If, somehow, through my suffering, my character, becomes more like Jesus' character and I learn to place my hope in the unswerving character of God, then it is all worth it.

The Therapy of Service

Corrie Ten Boom understood suffering. In a Nazi concentration camp for years, she lost her whole family while she was there. This is what Corrie Ten Boom has to say about how to persevere: "If you are unhappy with your lot in life, build a service station on it." What wisdom! I did not find this quote until much later in my widowhood, but God had already shown me that even during that first year of life without Mark, that I would shrivel up and blow away if I were unable to be a part of some ministry to others. I was given the opportunity to be a part of the Officers Christian Fellowship at the Air Force Academy, where I had come to know Christ thirteen years earlier. There I was able to lead Bible studies with the

148

female cadets and to open my home to provide them with a safe place to hang out. Their presence blessed me more than anything I could have offered them.

Later, I was given the opportunity to become a Shepherding home for the local pregnancy center. Young women in crisis pregnancies could come live with me for a year so I could be there for them to carry and deliver their babies, and then help them to get on their feet, financially, after the birth. My whole family was blessed through this ministry. We came to know and love the women who stayed with us. Both of these ministry opportunities allowed me to be outside of my own grief and focus on the needs of others. But while suffering can give us an opportunity for service, it can also give us a real connection to our Savior.

Participating in Jesus' Suffering

If I am able to identify with the sufferings of Christ more through my own suffering of trials, I will understand at a new level what He endured on my behalf. As my respect for the undeserved suffering He bore for me grows, so will the depth of my love for Him.

"I want to know Christ and the power of his resurrection and the fellowship of sharing in his suffering, becoming like him in his death, and so, somehow to attain the resurrection of the dead. Philippians 3:10-11

While the suffering I have endured is nothing next to the torment ruthlessly inflicted on Jesus, I understand His sacrifice for me a little better because of the emotional pain I have experienced.

Character produces hope. What should we place our hope in? In scripture, God does not promise me a new

149

husband, but He promises something much better, Himself:

> *"Keep your lives free from the love of money and be content with what you have, because God has said:*
> *'Never will I leave you;*
> *Never will I forsake you.'"*
>
> *Hebrews 13:5*

Relationships in this life come and go, but the one relationship that endures always is between God and me. The value of my life and the hope I have hinge on this one relationship.

The Value of Regrets

The week before Mark died on the same ski trip that allowed me to pronounce the depth of my love for Mark, we also had another argument. This one did not turn out as beautifully as the other one. It was not a knock down drag out argument, but I was upset with a situation and Mark felt as if there were more to it. "I do not feel like you like me any more," he said to me. Those words have burned the deep wound of regret in my soul. I *did* like him, he was my very best friend, but he was not feeling it. "The children are my focus right now," I told him, "I think it is just how things have to be while they are so young and while they demand so much of me physically." I have rehearsed a thousand lines I could have used to tell him he was my best friend and to reassure him that he was my favorite person on this earth. But I did not take the time to meet the need he was revealing to me. Instead, I made excuses for how I was treating him. Even now, many years later, as I write this, the pain of my regret is real and physical. I would love to have those moments in my life back to rewrite them. But they are lost forever.

How does this sad story of regret fit in the chapter on savoring the season? How do we move past the pain of regret to accept the present? It is among the greatest lessons from this book. It is not a lesson about exerting our will power, but rather tapping into the redemptive powers of God. *God does not give us the past to do again, but He gives us the future to live for Him.* **Regrets experienced early in life are a gift from God. They teach more poignantly than any other experience on this earth, how to savor the here and now, because tomorrow may never come.** I am a better parent from having lost Mark, because I realize I could lose one of my children just as tragically and just as suddenly as I lost Mark. I want my children to know each moment of each day of their lives that I love them and that I like them too. But this extends past just my children to my family, to my friends and to my acquaintances. It is my desire to make sure I live on loving terms with those I love, so regrets will have no part in my future. God has redeemed the pain of regret and taught me the joy of savoring the season.

When I look back on my childhood, I can see that I wasted much of it wanting to be older than I was. As an parent, I find myself telling my children over and over again, "appreciate this time in your life, you'll only be a child once." Yet, even with the wisdom of those words for my children, I find I want to rush out of this phase of my life. But unlike my childhood, I do not want to look back and see that I wasted this period of my life by wishing it away. I long to sit down, right where God has me, and learn all He has for me to learn, *no regrets, no wasted time.*

A Final Word

I have pressed on through the initial deep consuming pain of my loss, until graciously, the pain is now mostly a memory. I have pressed in to God to find real, practical faith in a powerful God. And I have pressed up to see my loss from God's eyes so I can be sure not to miss all He has planned for me through my grief. Looking back, of this I am sure: that I hear God better because of the trial. If I had the opportunity, I would not go back to who I was before. My ear was deaf to the voice of God. The trial has tuned my ear to hear His voice better.

Your story will be different from mine. What you hear God saying may be different. The important thing is taking the time to listen to God for yourself. I am eager to learn how God has met all your needs as you seek to hear his voice. I will be praying for you on your journey.

"Press"

A Season to Savor

As I rub my child's back, and she drifts off to sleep,
I realize there will soon come a day that she won't need me
A day when she'll be too big to let me rub her back.
And tears come to my eyes.

How did she get so big?
When did her chubby little body become so long and lean?
I realize that I have wished her infancy away, hoping each stage will
      be better.
And tears remain in my eyes.

Gone are the days of holding my infant close to my body.
Nevermore will she rely on my body for nourishment.
A season of her life has passed, and I did not have time to savor it.
And tears flow freely now.

It seems like I have trouble just keeping up with life.
There are so many things that seem important to get done each day.
But how can they be more important than savoring this season of my
      daughter's life?
And the tears become sobs.

Lord, help me to see the beauty of your creation, my daughter.
Help me take time to relish the sweetness of her youth.
May I savor each day I have with her, as if it were the last.
And through my tears, God gave me wisdom.

Summer '96

153

My dear child,

 I know you are confused, hurt, scared, and unsure of Me right now. So I'm writing to reassure you of My love for you. I thought of you before I put the world on its axis, and began it spinning. Before I breathed life into Adam, I knew your heart and loved you. I have seen your walk with me, how sometimes you're thrilled to be in my presence and sometimes you seem to have too much to do to spend time with me. I've seen you cry out to me in anger and pain over the last few days, and I hear you. I am crying with you. I know what your pain feels like, I've been there myself. I'm writing to ask you to trust me. Trust that I can see the bigger picture and all eternity is in my hands. Trust that my plan for you is better than you can imagine or hope for. Trust that I will walk every step of the journey ahead with you.

 You are My ambassador to My lost children. Through this trial, they will see My strength, My peace and My joy. If you let them, they will see that I am real. As you walk through the trials before you, I am with you. When you stumble, I will pick you up; when you weep, I will weep; when you find joy, I will rejoice with you; and when you are victorious, I will celebrate with you. Through this trial, I am drawing you unto Me. I want nothing more than for our hearts to be one. No obstacle is too high and no valley too deep for us to pass through together.

 I know the road seems rough and ugly in front of you. Trust Me to be your guide, your companion, your friend and your lover. I delight in caring for you. If you hold tightly to all you know to be true about Me, and step out in faith, I will be there for you in ways you have not experienced before.

 I will never leave you nor forsake you.

 The lover of your soul, always and forever,

   I AM

Appendix B

Ten Week Bible Study

WEEK ONE:

Read chapter 1, "Pressure Points: God's Fingerprints."

1. Read Jesus' words in Matthew 10:29-31. Do you understand and believe the value God places on you and your loved ones? Spell it out for yourself.

2. If "Not one [sparrow] of them will fall to the ground apart from the will of your Father," what does this say about the loss of your loved one?

3. What fingerprints can you see that God left in maneuvering both you and your loved one to where you were when your loved one died? Take the time to write them out.

4. Does contemplating that God was behind the scenes in the death of your loved one make you angry with God or does it bring you comfort? Write out your thoughts to God.

5. In what ways have you been "graciously humbled" by God or have you humbled yourself before God? What was the result in your spiritual life?

6. Read the statement in bold on the top of page seven again. What would change in your life if you really believed this?

      a. List the gifts God has given you to use for His purposes. How do they bring God glory?

      b. List the inadequacies you feel God has given you. How can God use these for His glory?

7. How has God used "bumps in the road" to help you grow? Would you have grown if God had answered your prayers as you prayed them?

8. The death of your loved one has shown you that life is short. What impact does that have in your day to day living?

9. If you have not already done so, write out everything you can remember about the story of your loved one's life and death.

WEEK TWO:

Read Chapter 2, "Hard Pressed: God Amidst the Turmoil"

1. Read in Matthew 26: 36-46 about Jesus' last moments in the garden of Gethsemane, just before he was arrested. Can you relate to the turmoil in His spirit? Have you brought your true fears and protests to God over the death of your loved one as Jesus did over His own death? What was the result?

2. Think back to your reaction to learning of your loved one's death. How did you react? How would you liked to have reacted? What is the difference?

3. How was God at work through and around the circumstances of your loved ones' death? How is He still at work?

4. In what ways does God use death to open doors for the gospel? List as many as you can think of.

5. In your own experience, did you see God's protective hand over the heart of anyone during the initial tumultuous stages of grief? Write what you saw.

6. Many are surprised at how physical grief can become. What purposes could God have behind this?

7. Jeremiah wrote a book about his grief over the nation of Israel, called Lamentations. Read chapter three and see if you can discover his source of optimism.

8. Reread the poem "Desperately Seeking Comfort." How does God provide comfort through grief to the believer? Write out ways God comforted you and is still doing so.

9. What is God using as reminders to you that "life goes on, somehow?"

WEEK THREE:

Read Chapter 2, "Pressure Cooker: Big Changes."

1. As life brings changes, so much more so does death.
Grief involves more than just mourning over the loved one
lost, but also mourning other things that must change as a
result of the loved one's death. Write out the major and
secondary changes you have faced since the death of your
loved one.

2. Bring each of the above changes to God and allow Him
to shed light on each one of them. He knows about them
already, but we need to know that He knows and cares
about them. Listen carefully for God's voice.

3.   As with the changes, there are also thoughts and
worries that we have. God knows about and cares for
these as well. Bring those to the One who knows
everything, anyway. Clean your soul by revealing
especially the thoughts and fears you think you have
hidden.

4. Describe in your words the difference between asking and whining. What difference does it make how we bring our questions to God?

5. Read the timeless words of Solomon, in Proverbs 4: 7-9. Whose wisdom is supreme? Who needs it? How do we get it?

6. Has losing a loved one pushed you to contemplate your own death? What has God shown you through those thoughts?

7. Can you see how God was there for you as you made logistical arrangements following the death of your loved one? Write those out as well, so you can thank God for them and use them as a reminder of God's faithfulness to you.

8. Read 2 Corinthians 7:4-7. Paul mentions what a comfort and encouragement Titus was to him. Is there one person, in particular, who has comforted and encouraged you during your grief? Have you thought of him or her as being sent to you by God? Write him or her a thank you letter.

WEEK FOUR:

Read Chapter 4, "Impressed by God: Finding Legs of Faith."

1. Read Matthew 14:27-33. What shows us in this story that Peter had "little faith?" Verse 30 says "when he saw the wind," so we know he lost sight of Jesus. What happens when you lose sight of Jesus?

2. Read Matthew 16:1-12. What was the "yeast of the Pharisees" from verse one that Jesus wanted them to guard against? What is wrong with asking God for a sign?

3. Read Matthew 17:19-21. Once again, Jesus is rebuking the disciples for their "little faith." Why does Jesus rebuke his disciples so harshly for this?

4. If you were to face Jesus today, what would he say about your faith? What limits your faith?

5. What does it mean to stand on our faith and burn all our other bridges? What "bridges" do you keep in life in case God does not hold you?

6. What hopes do you need to let go of? With what hopes can you replace those?

7. Pick one of the verses of promise from God on pages 63-70 or pick one of your own verses to memorize. Write it here:

8. Do you believe that God is pragmatic? What ways can you step out in faith to allow Him to show you that He will keep His promises?

9. Honestly assess yourself: Is there anything that you have tried to fill the void caused by the loss of your loved one with in your life with that is unhealthy or sinful?

10. If it is true that "a faithful heart is the venue God uses to display His miraculous powers" then what needs to change in your life to allow God the freedom to do the work He longs to do?

WEEK FIVE:

Read Chapter 5, "The Power Press: God's Omnipotence"

1. Read Matthew 22: 23-33. What was the Sadducees'
error? Do we still make this error today? What are the
consequences?

2. What areas of your life do you "but still" God? Write
out an "and" statement for each area.

God's word:	My "but still" Statement	My "and" Statement

3. What has God said that does not make sense in your life
right now? Can you believe Him? What steps will you
need to take so your life shows you believe God can do
that?

4. Think of a time that you stepped out in obedience and in doing so, you understood God better and His truths were made clearer to you. Write about it.

5. Do you believe that God has a policy of "no fault" questions or do you walk on eggshells around Him? What "no fault" questions would you like to bring to God?

6. How does understanding that God defines love, justice, mercy, goodness, righteousness, wisdom and truth change the way you might approach God when you have a question about one of these?

7. If God is love, what does that make all the things we think are love?

8. If God defines justice, how does that apply to the death of your loved one?

9. If God, Himself is the worthwhile end after which we strive in this world, how should that affect our day to day priorities?

WEEK SIX:

Read Chapter 6, "Compressed from Above: Ways of the Father."

1. Can you think of a story where what seemed awful and unfair was used by God for something of eternal significance? Write about it.

2. Is there anyone who can say he saw God clearer because he watched you face your loved one's death?

3. Do you believe that if you could go up and see the eternal picture that God sees that you would choose the path you are on? Talk to God about your doubts.

4. Read Hebrews 12:2-3. What do you think it means to keep your sights fixed on the "joy set before" you? How well do you do this? What needs to change so that you "will not grow weary and lose heart?"

5. What would this world be like if you ran it?

6. Read Habakkuk 3:17-19 again. Is it possible for you to "rejoice in the Lord" and be "joyful in God my Savior?" despite your circumstances?

7. Like Peter in Matthew 14, we flounder when we take our eyes off Jesus and put them on our surroundings. What part of your situation are you spending too much time focusing on? What practical steps can you take to refocus your mind on Jesus?

8. Read the poem "Designer Hands" again. If the death of your loved one was sifted through God's hand, what qualities of God can you look for despite your loss? Where have you seen those?

9. What does the "touch of the Designer's hand" look like in your life? Can you find it?

10. Thank God that it is He who is in charge, and not you. Praise Him for His attributes and acknowledge your limited vision, next to His. Confess the ways you have doubted Him and ask Him to help you trust Him.

WEEK SEVEN:

Read Chapter 9, "Expressing Gratitude: Thank You?"

1. Read I Thessalonians 5:16-18 again. Take an internal reading of your thankfulness. Are you "giving thanks in all circumstances?" Does God really expect us to?

2. Read Matthew 20:13-15. Think about the times you thought God was unfair. Was that based on His relationship to you or to others? Look again at that situation in light of the above verses. Does your view of God's fairness change?

3. What did the Father in the story of the prodigal son mean when he said "you are always with me, and everything I have is yours?" (Luke 15:31) What does that mean to you?

4. Do you believe that we deserve death for our sin? What difference should that make on how we view the hand God deals us?

5. How have your rights become a stumbling block preventing you from living powerfully? How can you become free from rights?

6. Make an extensive list of the undeserved gifts God has given you.

7. What is required before thankfulness can become a way of life?

8. If thankfulness is a choice, what do you choose? What practical steps will you take to make your life thankful?

9. What ways does having a thankful attitude benefit to us?

10. Read the poem, "Thanks Living" again. From where does our thankful attitude originate?

WEEK EIGHT:

Read Chapter 8, "Full Court Press: Persevering"

1. Life is tiring, even more so when experiencing grief. Write about the times you feel most tired and want to give up.

2. Read Romans 5:1-5 again. When you suffer, do you tend to persevere or faint and give up? Can you see how persevering has built your character? Write about it and thank God for it.

3. What hopes and dreams died with your loved one? Bring those to God and mourn them. Then look for the hope He wants to give you to replace them.

4. What do you hope in and hope for in this life and the next?

5. How can hope spring from a person who takes the time to spend time with God daily? Are you willing to give Him the opportunity to permeate your spirit with the living waters of His hope?

6. If the definition of a maturing character is one who is in the process of replacing his will with the will of the father, are you a maturing Christian? In what areas of your life have you seen God replacing your will with His?

7. How does it change your perspective to think of your emotions as "handwritten invitations from God?"

8. Have you found the body of Christ helpful in your situation? Have you reached out and asked for help? How are you being Christ's body to others?

9. What are you waiting on from God? Can you rest in God's timing for God's purposes?

10. Reread "The Weight of a Footprint". What "footprint" has God asked you to leave in this world today?

WEEK NINE:

Read Chapter 9, " God's Press Corps: Giving Glory to God."

1. Would God have the kind of confidence in you that He had in Job? How can you show God He did well in trusting you with this trial?

2. Can you see the platform God gave you through the loss of your loved one? How have you or how can you use this for his glory?

3. Can you see your trial as an honor that God would trust your heart? Thank God for the undeserved honor.

4. When are you weakest? Can people see God's strength through those times?

5. Have you had any "Peter Alerts" go off in your head as you have not given God the credit for what He has done? How can you be sure the next time that God gets the honor?

6. Has God brought others into your life with whom you have been able to share the comfort God has given you? Have you been faithful to point those to the Great Comforter?

7.   Describe in your own words the difference between seeking God's face and his hand.

8. Read Isaiah 61:1-3. Do you believe that God is able to "bestow a crown of beauty instead of ashes," " the oil of gladness instead of mourning" and "a garment of praise instead of a spirit of fear"? How is He doing this in and through your life?

9. How is God using you as an "oak of righteousness, a planting of the Lord for the display of His splender"? How will He? Name specifics.

10. Read the poem "Face Down" again. Have you ever really been face down (physically and spiritually) before the Lord? Spend some time in private face down before Him now.

WEEK TEN:

Read Chapter 10, "Wine Press: Savor the Season."

1. Jesus lost someone who meant a great deal to him at a young age as well. Read about John the Baptist's beheading and Jesus' response in Matthew 14: 6-23. Jesus did two things while He was mourning. What were they?

2. If Jesus needed "alone time" with God when He was in mourning, don't you think we do all the more? How are you getting that?

3. Reread the poem, "My Daddy's Lap." Do you see God as loving you like that? Write out ways you know God loves you.

4. How has your loss brought you to a place where you know and trust God more?

5. Read about Jesus' desert experience in Matthew 4: 1-11. Satan tempts us when he thinks we are the weakest. Jesus showed that God's strength can shine the brightest when we are weak. What was Jesus' "bread" while in the desert? What should ours be?

6. None of us particularly likes our "lot in life" when it comes to the loss of our loved ones. How can you, as Corrie Ten Boom suggested, "build a service station on it"?

7. How have you been able to identify with the sufferings of Christ more through your suffering?

8. Honestly assess your regrets with your loved one. How can God use these for His purposes?

9. What ways has God shown you that you need to savor the season you are in?

10. What ways have you learned to hear God better through your grief? Write them out.

About the Author

Patti McCarthy Broderick was born Patti MacGregor to Harry and Terry MacGregor. She graduated from Rockbridge High School, Rockbridge County, Virginia in 1981. She earned a B.S. in Civil Engineering when she graduated from the United States Air Force Academy in 1985. In 1994, as Patti McCarthy, she obtained a M.Ed. in counseling from Boston University. Currently, Patti is attending a doctoral program in counseling at Liberty University.

In 1999, Patti met Terry Broderick, father of two children and widower of Sheri Broderick, who died at age 33 of breast cancer. Patti and Terry were married in the summer of 1999 and now have five children together, Tiffani Broderick, Chris Broderick, Bryan McCarthy, David McCarthy and Christi McCarthy. All seven reside in Leesburg, Virginia.

Patti has been a Bible teacher and a conference speaker in several parts of the country. But her greatest passion is following Christ, which she has been privileged to do since 1982.